my CUISIQUE *vegetable* SPIRALIZER

COOKBOOK

101 Recipes to Turn Courgette into Pasta, Cauliflower into Rice, Potatoes into Lasagne, Beetroot into Salad with your CUISIQUE 4-Blade Spiral Slicer!

J.S. Amie

HHF Press
San Francisco

Legal Notice

The information contained in this book is for entertainment purposes only. The content represents the opinion of the author and is based on the author's personal experience and observations. The author does not assume any liability whatsoever for the use of or inability to use any or all information contained in this book, and accepts no responsibility for any loss or damages of any kind that may be incurred by the reader as a result of actions arising from the use of information in this book. Use this information at your own risk.

The author reserves the right to make any changes he or she deems necessary to future versions of the publication to ensure its accuracy.

Praise From Readers...

"This is a great book for vegetable spiralizer owners, and people who are interested in substituting vegetable "pasta" in place of traditional wheat pasta. The author, J.S. Amie, seems to have a good following on Amazon, and after reading this book I can see why!"

- Michelle G.

"My son has Celiac disease so we have to get creative in avoiding gluten. The Spiralizer really helps but the problem is, I'm just not that creative in the kitchen! My son isn't crazy about straight up string courgette which is where this book comes in. It offers inventive and creative recipes that I never would have come up with and my son (who is 11) will actually eat without complaint. He still seems to complains about everything else."

- Ryan J.

"Really happy with this book. Not only do you get delicious recipes, but you also can instruction on how to properly use your Spiralizer. I am trying to limit my gluten and wheat intake and my diet is mostly Paleo at this point, so these recipes are perfect!"

- Mary T.

"Its a very handy book to have. It gives suggestions on what kind of vegetables and fruits to use and how to clean your spiralizer."

- Renee I.

"This is a great intro into spiralizers. It has some great healthy gluten free, paleo and weight loss recipes. The Chicken Curry with Cauliflower "Rice" is on the menu tonight!"

- Dip F.

"Great book with quick and easy recipes. I was disappointed that the spiralizer itself didn't come with any type of book, but I'm glad I ordered this."

- Hammer

GET THE QUICKSTART GUIDE FREE!

This book comes with a spiralized vegetable quickstart guide which includes:

- Which vegetables to use

- Pro spiralizing techniques

- Gluten-free, paleo, and weight-loss pantry charts

- Free recipe resources

We've found that readers have more success with our book when they use the quick start guide. Download it today...absolutely free! See Chapter 3 for details.

DO YOU LIKE FREE BOOKS?

Every month we release a new book, and we offer it to our current readers first...absolutely free! This helps us get early feedback before launching a book, and lets you stock your shelf full of interesting and valuable books for free!

Some recent titles include:

- The Complete Vegetable Spiralizer Cookbook

- 101 The New Crepes Cookbook

- The Complete Food Dehydrator Cookbook

To receive this month's free book, just go to

http://www.healthyhappyfoodie.org/a5-freebooks

Table of Contents

What's In This Book

This book is the fourth book in a series of recipe books featuring "spiralized" vegetables as substitutes for pasta and other traditional ingredients. When I purchased my first vegetable spiralizer, I was excited to try making courgette noodles, also known as "zoodles." My first dish — courgette spaghetti with fresh tomatoes, basil and garlic — was fun, creative, and delicious! I quickly found that zoodles were popular with my friends and family. Everyone seemed pleasantly surprised by the experience and enthusiastically asked for more!

But when I began looking for recipes to satisfy my family's cravings for more, I couldn't find any! There were a few recipes here and there in popular Gluten-free cookbooks, but the recipes were uninspired, and did not fully capture the variety of flavors, textures and uses for this revolutionary way of preparing vegetables.

Additionally, I found very little in the way of "how to" instructions and advice for using these handy kitchen tools. I noticed that many people were having difficulties choosing the right vegetables for optimum results. I also read complaints from people who wanted to know how to handle the cutters correctly and safely. Hint: if you use them correctly, they won't bite!

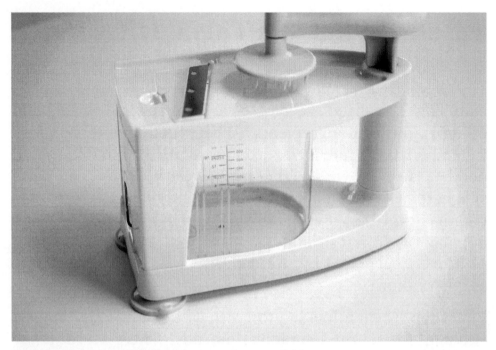

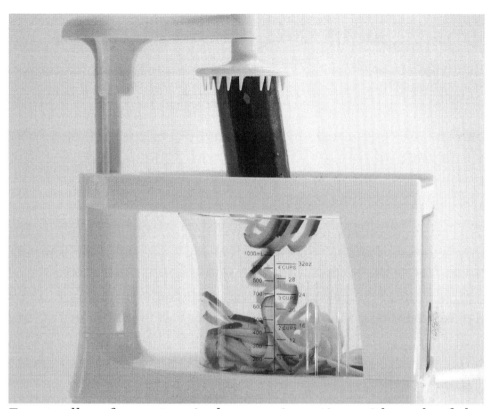

Eventually, after extensively experimenting with each of the most popular spiralizers (such as the Paderno, Veggetti and Cuisique Spiralizers), as well as various julienne peelers, I realized it was time to share my experience with others and hopefully inspire cooks everywhere to see for themselves how absolutely divine zoodles can be!

Who This Book Is For

Vegetable spiralizers were made to help people live healthier lives by replacing wheat in their diets while increasing the amount of vegetables they eat. Anyone who is trying to cut wheat out of his or her diet will immediately see the possibilities that open up when you have the ability to make your own delicious vegetable pasta substitutes.

The popular Cuisique Spiralizer is perfect for food lovers on any kind of regimen, including Gluten-Free, Paleo or weight-loss diets. This book will not only give you great recipes to utilize your new vegetable cutter, but it will show you how to use this utensil safely and efficiently.

The CUISIQUE SPIRALIZER

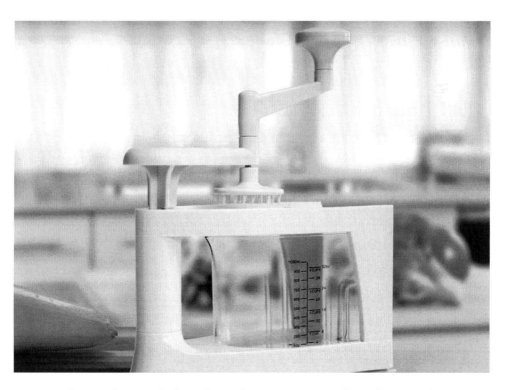

Using the right tool for the job is—as any handyman/woman knows—the key to success; you don't use a hammer to tighten a screw.

The Cuisique Spiralizer is a hand-powered tool, which means it is neither battery-powered nor electrical. About the size of a counter-top mixer, it is safer than other hand-held vegetable spiralizers, such as the Veggetti, because the vegetable is inserted into the machine, and directed toward the cutting blades by the action of a turning crank—the cook's hands never get anywhere near the sharp surfaces.

The Cuisique Spiralizer has several advantages over other popular spiralizers — more blades, more ways to slice, and a self-contained measuring cup — but the primary advantage is the ability to push downwards while spiralizing, whereas other spiralizers require more hand strength.

HERE'S HOW TO USE THE CUISIQUE SPIRALIZER SAFELY:

STEP 1: Make certain the machine is firmly "seated" on the counter and that the two suction cups at the back of the machine are "engaged." You do this by simply pushing down on the Cuisique's back end. Put your body into it! To release the suction, simply break the seal by pushing a finger under the suction cups.

STEP 2: Select the appropriate blade depending on how you want to process your vegetable or fruits. There are four blades provided with this slicer. Choose whether to use the Cuisique as a Spiralizer or as a Mandoline. *Carefully* attach the selected blade to the body of the Cuisique Spiralizer according to how you want to use it. Keep your fingers away from the blade at all times!

Spiralizer: orient the blade so it is inline with the crank. Sandwich the vegetable between the crank and the blade, being careful to center the vegetable over the little spike at the bottom of the blade.

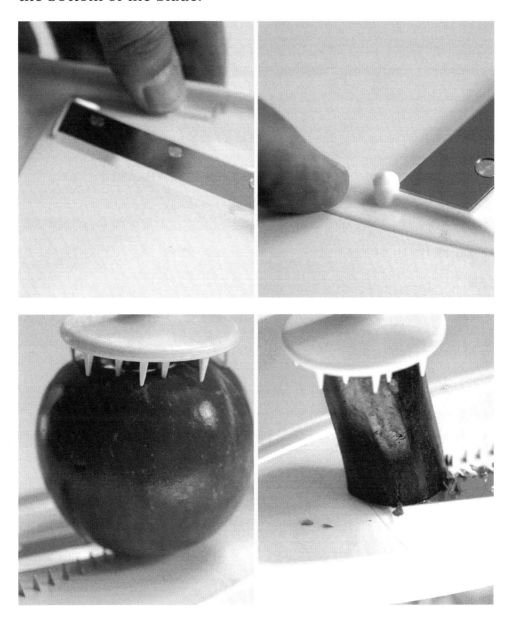

Mandoline: orient the blade perpendicular to the body of the Cuisique. Use the Cuisique's food safety holder and carefully slide the vegetable across the blade toward the back of the machine.

WARNING: Please keep your hand and fingers away from the blade while using the Cuisique as a mandoline. Use the Cuisique's included food safety holder to push a vegetable across the mandoline blade.

Warning: use the Cuisique's included food safety holder when using the Cuisique as a mandoline. Look at the photo below: it's easy to take a slice of finger along with courgette.

Quirks: Some vegetables may need to be trimmed a bit so that it will easily fit into the center blade.

STEP 3: Continue slicing or spiralizing until you reach the desired quantity. The Cuisique's handy container has level indicators just like a measuring cup!

BEST VEGGIES TO USE WITH THE CUISIQUE SPIRALIZER:

The Cuisique Spiral-Ultra Spiralizer is particularly good with soft and less dense vegetables and can easily handle larger vegetables that have a diameter of up to 5 inches.

- **Apples** —particularly nice for either spiralized or julienned cuts.

- **Potatoes** —either spiralized or julienned cuts.

- **Courgette** —terrific for either spiralized or julienned cuts.

- **Yellow Squash** —also terrific if the squash is large enough.

- Larger vegetables (up to 5 inches in diameter)

How To Clean Your Cuisique Spiralizer

The number one easiest way to clean each of these wonderful spiralizing tools is to wash them under running water immediately after use. If you wash immediately after using, then any vegetable matter will easily slough off of the tool and its blades. Warm soapy water is more effective as it softens the vegetable matter even more. Simply run water over the blades, and use your kitchen brush if needed, then put the tool on your drying rack. The entire process takes 30 seconds.

If you don't clean your spiralizer right away, then you'll have some extra work to do. The Cuisique Spiralizer blades and container are dishwasher-proof, so for the most part, all you need to do is throw them in the dishwasher and hit "go." But there are times when particles of vegetable matter will cling to the blades. When that happens, there are two easy ways to clean out the debris without putting your fingers at risk.

One method is to use hot water with the sink power sprayer to force the particles out. The second is to use a clean toothbrush to gently scrub the sharp surfaces. (Buy them by the handful at the pound shop and keep a couple in your utensil drawer. You'll be amazed at how useful they'll be.)

ALL ABOUT VEGETABLES

Not all vegetables and fruits work with each blade. For example, a tomato can be sliced by the mandoline blade, but it would turn to mush with a spiralizer blade. Nor can you spiralize vegetables and fruits with pits (avocados, stone fruits).

You can't spiralize vegetables that are smaller than 1½ inches in diameter. That category would include asparagus, green beans, and Chinese long beans. Very soft ingredients—like bananas—also don't work well in a spiralizer-type cutter, and neither will fruits like kiwi and watermelon that are mostly water. But again, the mandolin-style slicers work fine for these vegetables or fruits.

WHAT ARE THE BEST VEGETABLES (AND FRUITS) TO SPIRALIZE?

Here is a list of vegetables and fruits that I've found spiralize well:

Apples

Best way to slice: Slice using either spiralizer or mandoline mode, Apples range from tart to super sweet and any of the blades will work well with them. For best results, use firm apples without any soft spots. Leave the peel on to add a bit of color to the noodles.

Cooking tips: best eaten raw or baked.

Beetroot

Best way to slice: Beetroot are dense, hard vegetables and can be difficult to spiralize safely. I recommend using the mandoline mode instead of spiralizing, because of the difficulty in keeping the beet centered during spiralizing.

Cooking tips: Beetroot can be eaten raw, or cooked. Let the recipe or your own inspiration guide you.

Bell peppers

Best way to slice: Use the mandoline mode, whose precise cuts make for a professional presentation in dishes as diverse as sukiyaki and salads.

Cooking tips: They can be eaten raw or cooked.

Broccoli

Best way to slice: Use mandoline mode for the fibrous stalks. It is also possible to use the spiralizer mode to make the broccoli head into "rice", though it is a little tricky.

Cooking tips: The fibrous stalks of broccoli are perfect for short veggie pasta but they should be blanched before eating to cut down on the strong taste.

Cabbage

Best way to slice: Use a small cabbage head in mandoline mode. The different blades will produce thinner or thicker shreds.

Cooking tips: It can be eaten raw, but steaming the vegetable makes it particularly effective for lowering cholesterol.

Cauliflower

Best way to slice: The "flat" blade in spiralizer mode is perfect for turning cauliflower into "rice" or "couscous."

Cooking tips: Cauliflower should be cooked before eating. Because the texture of cauliflower rice is important, I recommend following the recipe's cooking instructions.

Carrots

Best way to slice: Small carrots are best sliced in mandoline mode, while larger/thicker carrots can often be spiralized into nice curly noodles.

Cooking tips: Eat them raw (thin carrot noodles are delicious raw), warm them with sauce or in soup, or cook them briefly in boiling water.

Celeriac

Best way to slice: All methods of slicing work well with this vegetable.

Cooking tips: It can be eaten raw or cooked, and is often mashed as a substitute for potatoes on weight-loss diets.

Chayote Squash

Best way to slice: All methods of slicing can be used on this vegetable.

Cooking tips: It can be eaten raw or cooked and its extremely mild flavor makes it perfect for pasta dishes where a more assertively flavored noodle (like broccoli) would overpower the taste.

Citrus Fruit

All you'll get is pulpy juice if you try to spiralize citrus fruit. But the mandoline method of slicing is perfect for shaving precise slices on everything from a tiny kumquat to a ruby red grapefruit. Whether the slices are being used as an essential ingredient—in something like a tomato quiche or a pitcher of sangria—or a garnish for a platter of poached salmon, the citrus fruit adds more than a spark of taste,

Cucumber

Best way to slice: All methods of slicing can be used on this vegetable.

Cooking tips: Cucumbers can be eaten raw or cooked, peeled or intact.

Eggplant

Best way to slice: Mandoline slices make an excellent base for traditional recipes like moussaka and lasagne.

Cooking tips: Eggplant should not be eaten raw. Roasting is particularly delicious way of cooking eggplant. Some recipes are better if you salt the raw eggplant and let the water drain out prior to cooking.

Jerusalem artichoke

Best way to slice: All methods of slicing can be used on this vegetable.

Cooking tips: They can be eaten raw but may cause "gas" if eaten in that state.

Jicama

Best way to slice: All methods of slicing can be used on this vegetable.

Cooking tips: It can be eaten raw and is often sold as a street snack in Mexico, sprinkled with lime juice and chili powder.

Leeks

Best way to slice: Leeks make lovely ribbons of flat pasta that work well in soups, salads, and pasta dishes. Best is to use the mandoline method.

Cooking tips: Like other members of the allium family, leeks can be eaten raw, but the are best when cooked to al dente perfection. My favorite way of serving any size or shape of leek is blanched with a sprinkle of olive oil and French sea salt.

Onion

Best way to slice: All methods of slicing can be used on this vegetable.

Parsnip

Best way to slice: Like carrots, small parsnips are best sliced in mandoline mode, while larger/thicker parsnips can often be spiralized into nice curly noodles.

Cooking tips: Baking and roasting are my preferred ways to cook Parsnips.

Pear

Slicing up a pears for desserts like clafouti or pie is a lot faster using either spiralizer or mandoline modes. There's no need to peel the fruit, simply wash and dry well before beginning the slicing process. (Pear skins have three to four times the nutrient value of the rest of the fruit, and those nutrients include antioxidants, anti-inflammatory and anti-cancer substances.) Plantain

Best way to slice: Unlike their botanical cousins bananas, plantains are firm enough to stand up to any kind of veggie cutter.

Cooking tips: Plantains need to be cooked before eating. They can be pan-fried, grilled and baked.

Potatoes

Best way to slice: All methods of slicing can be used on this vegetable.

Cooking tips: Always cook potatoes before eating. Potato noodles can fall apart when boiled.

Pumpkin

Best way to slice: Pumpkin needs to be cut down before it can be spiralized. As long as you cut the pumpkin to a somewhat regular shape, it can be spiralized or sliced in mandoline mode.

Cooking tips: Baking and roasting are preferred ways to cook pumpkin noodles, but check the recipe for specifics.

Radishes

Best way to slice: Because radishes are so small, they're difficult to spiralize, however a mandoline slicer can easily produce beautifully thin slices or matchsticks.

Cooking tips: Radishes are excellent raw.

Squash

Best way to slice: Yellow squash is very easy to spiralize or slice with a mandoline. Other squashes can require cutting with a knife prior to spiralizing. My strong preference is to use yellow squash when possible, as the results are consistently wonderful with this commonly available squash.

Cooking tips: If it is fresh, yellow squash is sweet and delicious raw. However, it quickly develops a bitter taste when it is no longer fresh. Cook yellow squash lightly, or it will turn mushy and lose its wonderful texture and flavor. My preferred way to prepare squash is blanched with a little olive oil and sea salt.

Sweet Potato

Best way to slice: All methods of slicing can be used on this vegetable.

Cooking tips: Sweet potatoes should not be eaten raw. Boiling the noodles too long can cause them to fall apart.

Tomatoes

Best way to slice: You can't spiralize tomatoes but you can use a handheld mandoline to slice them paper thin.

Cooking tips: Tomatoes can be eaten raw or cooked. Tomatoes are botanically fruit and their juicy flesh is a rich source of lycopene, a nutrient that can—among other things—limit and repair sun damage on skin.

Turnip

Best way to slice: All methods of slicing can be used on this vegetable.

Yam

Best way to slice: All methods of slicing can be used on this vegetable.

Cooking tips: Yams should be peeled and cooked before eating as they contain toxins.

Courgette

Best way to slice: All methods of slicing can be used on this vegetable.

Cooking tips: Fresh courgette can be eaten raw, peeled or unpeeled. Often, if the recipe is a hot dish, simply mixing the raw courgette noodles with the hot ingredients will "cook" the courgette noodles enough to be perfectly and enjoyably "al dente." If you prefer your courgette noodles to be cooked longer, then I recommend blanching for a few minutes and removing the cooked noodles from the pot to prevent overcooking.

HOW TO PREPARE AND COOK YOUR VEGETABLE "PASTA"

Cooking your vegetable pasta is even easier than cooking traditional pasta! Here's how:

RAW

Most of the pasta you make from fruits and vegetables can be eaten raw. The exceptions are potatoes, sweet potatoes, and eggplant. Raw sweet potato contains an enzyme inhibitor that blocks the digestion of protein. Raw potatoes absorb bacteria from the soil and water (listeria, E. coli, and salmonella). They should be cooked before eating to destroy the bacteria. Raw eggplant contains a substance that inhibits the absorption of calcium and can also cause neurological and digestive problems.

Note: For most thin noodles made with soft vegetables (courgette, yellow squash), mixing the warm or piping hot sauce with the raw noodles "cooks" them to just the desired "al dente" firmness.

WARMED

Warm the pasta strands by microwaving them for a few seconds in a microwave-safe bowl or by quickly "blanching" them in hot water before serving. (To blanch, bring a large pot of water to a boil. When the water is boiling, drop the noodles in and continue to heat for anywhere from 30 seconds to 10 minutes, depending on the vegetable. (Soft vegetables like courgette or yellow squash take about 30 seconds; carrots take several minutes, beetroot can take as long as 10 minutes.)

BOILED

You will not need to "boil" your vegetable pasta unless you like the texture soft, bordering on mushy. Some vegetable pasta--white potatoes for instance--will simply fall apart after being boiled. An alternative cooking method would be "steaming," where the vegetable pasta is put in a wire steaming basket and cooked over boiling water without actually being immersed in it.

Soft vegetables like courgette need only be boiled for 1-2 minutes. Firmer vegetables like beetroot need to be cooked up to 10 minutes. Use your own judgment and cook according to your preferred softness or firmness!

TIP: if you undercook the pasta just a little, then drizzle with virgin olive oil, you'll never want to cook it any other way.

SAUTÉED

This is a simple technique for cooking the pasta and other ingredients quickly. The ingredients are placed in a pan—either a saucepan or a frying pan—with a little fat or oil and cooked over high heat. The trick with this method is to stir often to prevent the ingredients from burning.

STIR-FRIED

Stir-frying is a quick-cooking method that requires very little fat. The secret to successful stir-fries is pre-prep.

All the ingredients should be chopped or cut as needed so that everything will cook quickly. Woks are purpose-built for stir-frying, but any large, heavy frying pan will do as well.

HERE'S A QUICK PRIMER ON HOW TO STIR FRY:

Make sure your ingredients are dry.

- Heat the oil over high heat, then add the aromatic ingredients (garlic, chilis, onions) and spices to the oil before adding any other ingredients. This allows the flavors to infuse the oil.

- Add the rest of the ingredients, being careful not to overcrowd the pan. If necessary cook in small batches.

- As with sautéing, you need to pay attention to the process; stir-frying is done over high heat and the ingredients can easily burn.

BAKED

Pasta in traditional dishes like mac and cheese has to be boiled first before being combined with the cheese sauce and baked.

With vegetable noodles, you can simply add the raw noodles to the ingredients—they'll cook while the dish is baking, thus saving you a step. Keep in mind that vegetable noodles cook much more quickly than wheat pasta, therefore your baking times will be considerably shorter than usual.

Tip: pat your sliced or spiralized courgette noodles with paper towels to remove extra moisture. This will help keep your baked noodles from becoming too watery.

How Much "Pasta" Will It Make?

For most traditional pasta recipes, the default ingredient is 1lb o r 454 gms of pasta, which yields 4 cups of cooked pasta. In the following recipes, 4 cups of vegetable spaghetti will be the standard ingredient. To get 4 cups of vegetable pasta from your veggies use the following guide. Equivalents are approximate depending on the size of the vegetable.

- **Beetroot** :: 8 medium beetroot, trimmed = 4 cups beat pasta

- **Broccoli** :: 6-8 trimmed broccoli stalks = 4 cups broccoli pasta

- **Carrot** :: 8 medium carrots = 4 cups carrot pasta

- **Cauliflower** :: 1 head of trimmed cauliflower = 4 cups cauliflower "rice"

- **Cucumbers** :: 3-4 medium cucumbers = 4 cups cucumber pasta

- **Jicama** :: 2 whole jicamas = 4 cups jicama pasta.

- **Potato** :: 6 medium potatoes = 4 cups potato pasta

- **Radish** :: 2 Daikon radishes = 4 cups radish pasta

- **Squash** :: 4-6 yellow squash = 4 cups squash pasta

- **Sweet Potato** :: 3 medium sweet potatoes = 4 cups sweet potato pasta

- **Courgette** :: 3-4 whole courgette = 4 cups courgette pasta

HOW TO STORE LEFTOVER VEGETABLE PASTA

Leftover veggie noodles must be refrigerated, preferably in a container (glass or plastic) with an air-tight seal in the coldest part of the fridge. If the noodles have been cooked, or mixed with other hot ingredients, you can store them for up to 2 days. If the noodles are raw, they should be used within 24 hours. If you want to prevent discoloration, squeeze a little lemon juice over the raw pasta before storing.

HOW TO MAKE SPIRALIZED

NOODLES & RICE

Just as there are different pasta shapes to fit different dishes (you wouldn't serve a single flabby flat lasagne noodle with sauce poured over it) you can choose specific widths and lengths of spiral-cut vegetables to make your spiralized meal perfect.

CHOOSING THE RIGHT "NOODLE" OR "RICE" FOR THE DISH

Vegetable 'rice" made with a spiralizer can be used interchangeably with rice or couscous in dishes, whether served as a "side" or cooked with other ingredients as part of a more elaborate dish.

Thick, thin and curly/ring-shaped vegetables strands, however require a little more thought when pairing them up in more complex dishes. Generally speaking, you can use thick and thin vegetable strands in the same way you would use traditional ribbon cut pasta — with thinner strands working best for simple, light sauces such as marinara, and thicker strands for heavier meat sauces.

Spiralized "rings" make an especially fine base for vegetable "pasta" salads. They also work well for some dense vegetables, which are difficult to slice into strands, such as potatoes and beetroot.

Spiralized "crescents" work well with soups, as they can be easer to spoon than rings or strands.

Blade Chart

Thin Strands

Thin Rings

Thin Crescents

Thick Strands

Thick Rings

Thick Crescents

Flat Strands

Flat Rings

Flat Crescents

HOW TO MAKE "NOODLES" (THIN, THICK AND FLAT STRANDS)

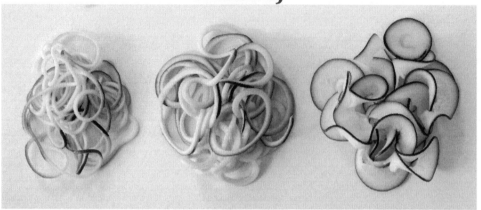

Noodles (strands) are the basic shape produced by spiralizing. If you're spiralizing something, then a long noodle will naturally come out the other end. Simply select your blade according to how thick you want your strands to be.

HOW TO MAKE "RINGS"

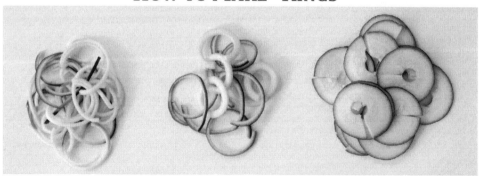

Rings are a little more complex than a simple strand, but still easy to make! Here's how:

- Choose an appropriate vegetable. Courgette, squash, potatoes, beetroot, cucumber, daikon and large carrots are all good candidates for making rings.

- Slit the vegetable along its length on one side. Make sure the slit doesn't reach the center of the vegetable.

- Spiralize the vegetable as usual, being careful since the vegetable will be a little weaker than without the slit.

HOW TO MAKE "CRESCENTS"

Crescents are a little more difficult because they make the vegetable weak and more difficult to spiralize without breaking. Nevertheless, once you get the hang of it, making crescents is actually easy. Here's how:

- Choose an appropriate vegetable. Courgette, squash, potatoes, beetroot, cucumber, daikon and large carrots are all good candidates for making rings.

- Slit the vegetable along its length on BOTH sides. Here it's extremely important to be careful how deep you make the slits. Try to avoid cutting into the core, as this will cause the vegetable to fall apart while spiralizing.

- Spiralize the vegetable carefully.

HOW TO MAKE "FLAT NOODLES"

Flat noodles are made by using the flat blade with the mandoline method instead of spiralizing. Simply set the flat blade perpendicular to the body of the Cuisique, remove the spiralizing crank, and run the vegetable lengthwise across the blade. Be sure to use the Cuisique's food safety holder so you don't cut yourself on the sharp blade!

HOW TO MAKE "RICE"

Making "rice" out of cauliflower and broccoli can be a little messy, but it's absolutely delicious and FUN! Here's how:

- Choose a small to medium-sized cauliflower. (If you're using broccoli, make sure it's firm and not wilted).

- Cut the stem off, you'll be spiralizing the head only.

- Use the flat blade on your Cuisique spiralizer.

- Spiralize the head of the cauliflower (or broccoli). The resulting chips and grains will be uneven in size, but the unevenness adds a nice texture to a surprising dish.

- Cook by boiling or sautéing. Cooked cauliflower (or broccoli) "rice" can be used as a delicious replacement for rice or couscous in just about any dish.

DOWNLOAD THE QUICKSTART GUIDE

This book comes with a Quickstart Guide which includes:

- Which vegetables to use

- Pro spiralizing techniques

- Gluten-free, paleo, and weight-loss pantry charts

- Free recipe resources

We've found that readers have more success with our book when they use the Quickstart Guide. Download it today, it's absolutely free!

To download your free QuickStart Guide, just go to: **www.healthyhappyfoodie.org/a4-quickstart**

SOUPS

Noodle soups are universally found throughout the world and are considered comfort food in any language. Starting a meal with a nutritious bowl of soup "takes the edge" off the appetite, and generally results in consuming less calories per meal, a boon for those watching their weight.

GF - Gluten-free

P - Paleo

WL - Weight-Loss

V - Vegetarian

Vg – Vegan

ASIAN PASTA WITH BROTH

In Japan, noodle shops are as ubiquitous as Starbucks, and for good reason. A hearty bowl of noodle soup with bits and pieces of vegetable, tofu and meat makes a cheap and satisfying meal. Go ahead and slurp— it's not considered impolite!

Prep Time: 15 m

Serves: 2

Calories: 319, Sodium: 1,719 mg, Dietary Fiber: 3.2 g, Total Fat: 22.4 g, Total Carbs: 10.9 g

INGREDIENTS

....

"PASTA"

2 large daikon radishes, spiralized

SOUP

1 cups bok choy, shredded (may substitute spinach)

1 12-oz. block firm tofu, drained and diced

2 Tbsp. dark sesame oil

½ cup sliced spring onions (reserve some for garnish)

2 garlic cloves, minced

1 Tbsp. fresh ginger, grated

2 cups stock, low-sodium

½ cup water

1 Tbsp. rice vinegar

2 tsp. soy sauce, low-sodium

Dash crushed red pepper flakes

....

DIRECTIONS

1. Spiralize the daikon radish (thin crescents recommended).

2. In a small frying pan, brown the diced tofu with 1 tablespoon oil over medium heat.

3. Throw the daikon crescents along with all ingredients into a medium saucepan and bring to a boil.

4. Boil for a few seconds, then turn off heat.

5. Serve hot, garnished with reserved green onion.

Note: for a different flavor, substitute 2-3 tablespoons of miso paste for the soy sauce.

CHICKEN "NOODLE" SOUP

The virtues of chicken soup have been celebrated in nearly every culture, and for good reason. This is a home-made version that "cheats" a little bit by using stock as a base, but it sacrifices nothing in nutrition.

Prep Time: 15 m

Serves: 2–4

Nutritional Info: Calories: 170, Sodium: 156 mg, Dietary Fiber: 3.9 g, Total Fat: 6.7 g, Total Carbs: 13.3 g, Protein: 14.5 g

INGREDIENTS

....

"NOODLES"

2 large carrots, spiralized

2 big bunches of broccoli (stems only), spiralized

SOUP

4 cups (1 quart) low sodium stock

8 cups water

2-3 skinless chicken breasts, diced

1 large onion, diced

2 minced garlic cloves

1 Tbsp. olive oil

2 tsp. curry powder

Dash red pepper flakes

....

DIRECTIONS

1. Combine the stock, water, garlic, onion, curry powder, and olive oil in a medium saucepan and bring to a boil.

2. Reduce heat to a simmer and cover.

3. In a non-stick pan, sauté the diced chicken pieces until they're white all the way through. (Be careful not to overcook the chicken.).

4. Spiralize the carrots and broccoli (thick crescents recommended).

5. Add the chicken and the vegetable noodles to the simmering soup.

6. Garnish with a dash of pepper flakes.

7. Simmer briefly until all the ingredients are heated through, about two minutes.

Note: Broccoli stem pasta strands taste great but don't "present" as well as other vegetable-based pastas. You can substitute courgette or any other squash strands in this dish.

CURRIED LEEK & LENTIL SOUP

Hardcore followers of the Paleo diet do not allow lentils on their menu as they are edible pulses that have been cultivated since the Neolithic era (roughly 13,000 years ago). At the same time, though, many who follow the "Caveman" diet make exceptions for dark chocolate, which is also post-Paleolithic, although it has been cultivated for 3,000 years. If you don't want to stray outside the lines, simply leave out the lentils and turn this into a lovely, curry-scented broth with vegetables.

Prep Time: 30–45 m

Serves: 8–10

Nutritional Info: Calories: 122, Sodium: 25 mg, Dietary Fiber: 7.4 g, Total Fat: 1.9 g, Total Carbs: 18.6 g, Protein: 5.8 g

INGREDIENTS

....

SPIRALIZED VEGGIES

3 large carrots, spiralized

2 large leeks (white parts only), spiralized

MAIN INGREDIENTS

1 Tbsp. olive oil

1 yellow onion, coarsely chopped

5 cloves garlic, minced

¼ tsp. ginger (1 Tbsp. if fresh grated)

2 Tbsp. curry powder

1 tsp. cumin

1 cup green lentils, rinsed (optional)

6 cups water

....

DIRECTIONS

1. In a large soup pot, sauté the onion in the olive oil over medium heat until translucent.

2. Spiralize the leeks into thick strands and the carrots into thin rings. Add them to the soup pot.

3. Sauté until the leeks are tender. (Carrots will still be slightly firm.)

4. Add the spices and stir so the vegetables are evenly coated.

5. Add the lentils and the water.

6. Cover the pot and bring to a boil.

7. Reduce heat and simmer for 10-15 minutes to blend flavors. If using lentils, simmer for 25-30 minutes until lentils are tender, stirring occasionally.

LOW CARB BEEF PHO

Considered the national dish of Vietnam, Pho is traditionally made with beef broth, sometimes enriched with oxtail. This is a simplified version that replaced flat rice noodles with veggie pasta.

Prep Time: 25–30 m

Serves: 4

Calories: 283, Sodium: 2279 mg, Dietary Fiber: 3.2 g, Total Fat: 10.1 g, Total Carbs: 10.8 g, Protein: 35.7g

INGREDIENTS

....

2 cups yellow squash, spiralized

8 cups beef broth, preferably low sodium

4 cups water

¾ pound flank steak, very thinly sliced

1 medium yellow onion, sliced

4-6 garlic cloves, minced

1 2-inch piece ginger root, grated

2 whole cloves

1 cinnamon stick

2 Tbsp. fish sauce

For garnish: chopped spring onions, thinly sliced jalapeno peppers, chopped coriander, lime wedges

....

DIRECTIONS

1. Combine broth, water, and spices in a large stockpot. Bring to a boil over high heat, then cover the pan and reduce the heat. Simmer for half an hour, stirring occasionally.

2. Spiralize the squash into thick strands.

3. Add the squash strands and beef to the pot, return to a boil just long enough to cook the beef, about 1-2 minutes if the beef is sliced very thin.

4. Remove the cinnamon stick, then serve hot with garnishes as desired.

MEXICAN CHICKEN NOODLE SOUP

GF | P | WL

This spicy, tomato-based soup is another international variation of chicken noodle soup.

Prep Time: 25–30 m

Serves: 6

Nutritional Info: Calories: 592, Sodium: 1336 mg, Dietary Fiber: 2.1 g, Total Fat: 33.4 g, Total Carbs: 46.5 g, Protein: 32.3 g

INGREDIENTS

....

2 cups courgette, spiralized

6 cups chicken stock

2 14-oz. cans roasted tomatoes

4 boneless, skinless chicken breasts

5 large garlic cloves, minced

1 yellow onion, chopped

1 large bunch coriander, chopped (approximately 1 cup)

1 jalapeno pepper, seeded and minced

2 medium carrots, chopped into "coins"

Juice of 2 limes

2 Tbsp. olive oil

1 tsp. cumin

1 tsp. turmeric

1 tsp. black pepper

....

DIRECTIONS

1. Spiralize the courgette into thin crescents.

2. In a large stock pot, heat the onion, carrots, and garlic in the oil until the onions are translucent.

3. Add the canned tomatoes (juice and all), the chicken stock and the chicken pieces. Bring to a boil and cook until the chicken is cooked through. Remove the chicken from the pot and set aside to cool.

4. Reduce to a simmer and cover. When the chicken is cool, shred it and return it to the pot, along with the noodles, the spices, and the line juice.

5. Continue to simmer for another 30 seconds, then remove from heat.

MINESTRONE

GF

One of the first Italian words a diner learns (right after "spaghetti," is "minestrone." This classic vegetable soup easily fits into any eating plan that embraces veggies. Note: Without the Parmesan garnish, this recipe is Paleo; substitute vegetable broth for the stock to make it vegan.

Prep Time: 6 h

Serves: 4–6

Nutritional Info: Calories: 356, Sodium: 810 mg, Dietary Fiber: 24.4 g, Total Fat: 2.0 g, Total Carbs: 61.7 g, Protein: 24.5 g

INGREDIENTS

....

1 cup courgette or yellow squash, spiralized

4 cups stock

1 28-oz. can crushed tomatoes

1 15.5-oz. can cannellini beans, drained and rinsed to remove excess salt

1 cup escarole or kale, shredded

2 large carrots, cut into "coins"

2 ribs celery, diced

1 large yellow onion, chopped

3 large garlic cloves, minced

2 tsp. Italian seasoning

Grated Parmesan cheese (optional)

....

DIRECTIONS

1. Spiralize the courgette or yellow squash into thin rings.

2. Combine the broth and the canned tomatoes (juice included) with the carrots, celery, garlic, and onion in a slow cooker. Stir in the Italian seasoning. (If using tomatoes that have "Italian seasoning" don't add more.)

3. Cover and cook on low for 4-6 hours, then add the escarole, and beans. Cover and increase heat. Cook for another 5-10 minutes, until the greens are wilted.

4. Add the noodles and cook another 1-2 minutes. Serve hot, garnished with Parmesan if desired.

PASTA E FAGILO

GF | P

This pasta and bean soup is another hearty, healthy example of "Mediterranean" cuisine. Substitute short, curly courgette noodles made with the Paderno for the traditional tiny tube-shaped pasta.

Prep Time: 45 m

Serves: 8

Nutritional Info: Calories: 549, Sodium: 1046 mg, Dietary Fiber: 24.2 g, Total Fat: 11.0 g, Total Carbs: 76.5 g, Protein: 38.9 g

INGREDIENTS

....

1 cup courgette or yellow squash, spiralized

1lb o r 454 gms spicy Italian sausage (if using links, remove casing)

4 cups stock

1 cup water

4 carrots, sliced into coins

1 large yellow onion, diced

4 garlic cloves, crushed

1 16-oz. can tomato sauce

1 15-oz. can diced tomatoes

1 15-oz. can kidney beans

1 15-oz can cannellini or navy beans

1 Tbsp. Italian seasoning

··

DIRECTIONS

1. Spiralize the courgette or yellow squash into flat crescents.

2. Crumble the sausage into the bottom of a large stockpot or Dutch oven and brown over medium heat. Drain off the excess fat and then add the olive oil, garlic, onions, and carrots. Cook until the vegetables are tender (about 4 minutes). Stir occasionally.

3. Add the water, chicken stock, tomato sauce, and diced tomatoes (including juice). Stir in the Italian seasoning and bring to a boil.

4. Drain and rinse the canned beans, then add to the soup. Add the beans to the pot and reduce heat. Simmer for 2-3 minutes, then toss in the noodles and simmer another 1-2 minutes. Serve hot.

PUMPKIN NOODLE SOUP

GF | WL | V | VG

This soup combines rich fall flavors with an ease of preparation that will make it a favorite.

Prep Time: 25 m

Serves: 6

Nutritional Info: Calories: 150, Sodium: 645 mg, Dietary Fiber: 6.3 g, Total Fat: 6.3 g, Total Carbs: 19.3 g, Protein: 6.2 g

INGREDIENTS

....

4 cups pumpkin or squash, spiralized

5 cups vegetable broth

1 large (29-oz.) can pumpkin puree (not the pumpkin pie filling kind)

1 large yellow onion, diced

2 Tbsp. olive oil

½ Tbsp. brown sugar

2 tsp. sage (or 2 Tbsp. fresh sage, chopped)

1 tsp. cinnamon

¼ tsp. ginger

¼ tsp. cayenne pepper

1/8 tsp. nutmeg

....

DIRECTIONS

1. Heat the oil in a large saucepot and add the chopped onions. Cook until the onions are translucent, 3-5 minutes. Stir in the spices.

2. Add the pumpkin puree and the vegetable broth. Bring to a boil, then reduce to a simmer.

3. Stir in the brown sugar.

4. Add the pumpkin noodles (flat rings recommended) and simmer for another 2-3 minutes.

Note: Leave out the brown sugar to make this soup Paleo-friendly.

SHRIMP SOUP WITH BOK CHOY

GF | P | WL

This seafood soup is half a world away from the tomato-based seafood stews found in the Mediterranean.

Prep Time: 35–45 m

Serves: 6–8

Nutritional Info: Calories: 307, Sodium: 1066 mg, Dietary Fiber: 1.9 g, Total Fat: 8.3 g, Total Carbs: 27.5 g, Protein: 30.4 g

INGREDIENTS

....

3 cups courgette, spiralized

1 ½ cups fish stock (or seafood stock)

6 cups chicken stock

2 lbs. raw shrimp, cleaned, shelled, and deveined

1 large bok choy, trimmed and sliced thinly

3 spring onions, thinly sliced

1 Tbsp. crushed red pepper flakes

2 Tbsp. grated ginger

3 large garlic cloves, minced

1/3 lb. shiitake mushrooms, sliced

3 Tbsp. rapeseed oil

....

DIRECTIONS

1. Spiralize the courgette into flat crescents.

2. Heat the oil in a large stockpot and add the bok choy, mushrooms, garlic, ginger, and red pepper flakes. Heat on medium for a minute, then add the broth and fish stock. Cover the pot and bring to a boil.

3. Add the shrimp and sliced spring onions. Continue to cook for another 2 minutes, or until shrimp are cooked through.

4. Toss in the noodles, remove from heat and let stand 5 minutes before serving.

THAI CHICKEN NOODLE SOUP

GF | P | WL

This soup features three flavors that define Thai cuisine, coconut, chili, and lime.

Prep Time: 25–30 m

Serves: 4

Nutritional Info: calories: 378, Sodium: 1208 mg, Dietary Fiber: 2.4 g, Total Fat: 21.6 g, Total Carbs: 17.0 g, Protein: 30.0 g

INGREDIENTS

....

½ cup courgette, spiralized

2 boneless, skinless chicken breasts cut into bite-size pieces

5 cups stock

1 cup coconut milk (can use low-fat)

2 jalapeno peppers, seeded and chopped finely

2 large garlic cloves, chopped

1 ½ inch piece ginger root, grated

1 Tbsp. lime zest

¼ cup fresh lime juice

4 Tbsp. fish sauce (I use Red Boat)

2 cups shiitake mushrooms, sliced

2 cups baby spinach leaves

2 Tbsp. chopped coriander

....

DIRECTIONS

1. Spiralize the courgette into thin rings.

2. Combine the stock, jalapeno, garlic, ginger, lime juice and zest and 3 Tbsp. fish sauce in a medium sauce pan and bring to a simmer.

3. Add the courgette noodles and cook for one minute or until tender. Use tongs to remove the noodles. Place in a bowl and cover to keep warm.

4. Add the mushrooms to the simmering broth. Simmer for another four minutes, then add the chicken and the coconut milk.

5. Continue to simmer until the chicken is cooked through.

6. Add the spinach and stir until the leaves get limp, then add the chopped coriander and remaining tablespoon of fish sauce.

7. Divide the cooked noodles into four bowls and pour the soup over the noodles.

TUNISIAN NOODLE SOUP

GF | P | WL

This spicy noodle soup is a vegetarian African variation of the ubiquitous chicken noodle soup.

Prep Time: 25–30 m

Serves: 4–6

Nutritional Info: Calories: 181, Sodium: 184 mg, Dietary Fiber: 2.9 g, Total Fat: 10.0 g, Total Carbs: 20.7 g, Protein: 4.7 g

INGREDIENTS

....

2 cups courgette, spiralized

4 pints vegetable stock (or chicken stock)

1lb o r 454 gms Swiss chard, chopped coarsely (stems, ribs, and eaves)

1 large red onion, chopped

3 large garlic cloves, minced

4 Tbsp. olive oil (or coconut oil)

2 Tbsp. tomato paste

2 Tbsp. hot pepper sauce

1 Tbsp. fresh lemon juice

....

DIRECTIONS

1. Bring the stock to a boil in a stockpot. Add the chard and cook until the chard is wilted.

2. Stir in the tomato paste, oil, hot pepper sauce, garlic, and onion. Return to a boil and then reduce to a simmer.

3. Simmer for 5-10 minutes, then add the courgette noodles (thin rings recommended). Cook for about 1 minute, or until they are tender.

MISO NOODLE SOUP

GF | P | WL | V | VG

This light vegetable/noodle broth can serve as a first course or as a light lunch all by itself.

Prep Time: 25–30 m

Serves: 6–8

Calories: 159, Sodium: 692 mg, Dietary Fiber: 3.9 g, Total Fat: 6.1 g, Total Carbs: 20.2 g, Protein: 7.9 g

INGREDIENTS

....

1 cup courgette, spiralized

4 carrots, spiralized

3 quarts water

2 leeks, white part only, sliced

1 bunch Swiss chard (or black kale), about ½ pound

4 carrots, cut into chunks

3 garlic cloves, minced

2 spring onions, sliced

1 cup edamame (can use frozen)

½ cup miso paste

1 ½ Tbsp. olive oil

....

DIRECTIONS

1. Heat the oil in a large stock pot for 1 minute, then add the leeks and garlic. Cook over medium heat for another 5 minutes, stirring occasionally.

2. Separate the chard leaves from the ribs and stalks and set aside. Chop the ribs and stalks, then add to the leek and garlic mixture. Continue to cook until the chard is tender, 8-10 minutes. Stir occasionally so the vegetables don't stick.

3. Add the water to the pot and bring to a boil. Add the chopped carrots and reduce heat to a simmer. Simmer for 5 minutes or until the carrots are almost soft.

4. Spiralize the courgette (thin rings recommended) and carrots (thin strands recommended).

5. Chop the chard leaves and add to the soup along with the edamame. Simmer until the greens wilt, then bring to a boil.

6. Remove 1 cup of boiling water and add it to the miso paste. Add the miso mixture to the soup along with the noodles and return to a boil. As soon as the noodles are tender (about 30-60 seconds), remove from heat and serve. Garnish with sliced spring onions.

SALADS

At formal dinners salads are served as a separate course while at family-style meals they're usually served on the side. Hearty or light, warm or cold, these salads will add the finishing touch to your menu.

GF - Gluten-free

P - Paleo

WL - Weight-Loss

V - for Vegetarian

Vg – Vegan

BEET SALAD

This colorful, naturally sweet salad is eaten raw, unlike many roasted beet salads, which makes it quick and easy to prepare.

Prep Time: 5–10 m

Serves: 2

Nutritional Info: Calories: 315, Sodium: 117 mg, Dietary Fiber: 3.5 g, Total Fat: 28.5 g, Total Carbs: 16.4 g, Protein: 2.7 g

INGREDIENTS

....

RIBBONS

3 beetroot (about half a pound), spiralized

DRESSING

2 Tbsp. balsamic vinegar

4 Tbsp. olive oil

1 large garlic clove, minced

2 tsp. minced rosemary

....

DIRECTIONS

1. Wash and peel the beetroot. Spiralize into beautiful thin strands. Combine the rest of the ingredients and pour over the beetroot.

2. Toss to coat.

3. Serve immediately.

4. Note: You can make this with red beetroot alone, but in the spring, when baby golden beetroot are available, they make a colorful addition. Try substituting orange juice for the vinegar.

DILLED SALMON PASTA SALAD

GF

This is a good recipe to make a little salmon go a long way and a tasty alternative to the traditional tuna salad option.

Prep Time: 20 m

Serves: 6

Calories: 676, Sodium: 192 mg, Dietary Fiber: 4.0 g, Total Fat: 40.0 g, Total Carbs: 58.4 g, Protein: 24.5 g

INGREDIENTS

....

8 cups courgette, spiralized

1 15-oz can salmon, drained and flaked

1 bunch fresh dill, minced

2 bell peppers, seeded and minced (can use any color)

1 cup olive oil

1/3 cup Dijon mustard

½ red wine vinegar

2 garlic cloves, minced

....

DIRECTIONS

1. Blanche the courgette noodles (thick rings recommended) if a soft noodle is desired, otherwise leave uncooked.

2. Whisk the olive oil with the mustard, garlic, and vinegar in a large bowl.

3. Add the noodles, peppers, and salmon.

4. Toss to combine.

GREEK PASTA SALAD

GF | WL

The Greek flavors of this quick and easy pasta salad make a nice change from the more common "Italian" versions.

Prep Time: 15 m

Serves: 4–6

Calories: 410, Sodium: 537 mg, Dietary Fiber: 3.1 g, Total Fat: 27.0 g, Total Carbs: 33 g, Protein: 11.1 g

INGREDIENTS

....

4 cups courgette, spiralized

1 bunch spring onions, sliced

1 basket cherry tomatoes, halved

1 pkg. sliced white mushrooms

1 large bell pepper, seeded and sliced into matchsticks

1 4-oz. can pitted black olives, drained

¾ cup chorizo, thinly sliced

1 cup feta cheese, crumbled

2 large garlic cloves, minced

2 tsp. basil

1 ½ tsp. oregano

½ tsp. black pepper

½ cup olive oil

½ cup red wine vinegar

....

DIRECTIONS

1. Spiralize the courgette into thick rings.

2. Blanche the noodles if you desire a softer noodle. Otherwise leave raw.

3. In a large bowl, combine the oil, vinegar, garlic, basil, oregano, and pepper. Whisk to blend.

4. Add remaining ingredients, including noodles, and toss to distribute dressing evenly.

5. Chill overnight to blend flavors.

Note: *Leave out the chorizo to convert this to a vegetarian salad.*

JERUSALEM ARTICHOKE SLAW

GF | V

Cooked Jerusalem artichokes can sub for potatoes in a lot of dishes; served raw as they are here, they have a crisp texture reminiscent of water chestnuts.

Prep Time: 75 m

Serves: 4–6

Calories: 94, Sodium: 34 mg, Dietary Fiber: 1.0 g, Total Fat: 2.3 g, Total Carbs: 10.9 g, Protein: 7.8 g

INGREDIENTS

....

1 large carrot, spiralized

½ lb. Jerusalem artichokes, peeled, matchstick cut

2 Tbsp. sour cream

2 Tbsp. Greek yogurt

1 Tsp. dry mustard

2 tsp. white wine vinegar

¼ tsp. black pepper

....

DIRECTIONS

1. Chopped parsley (if desired) for garnish

2. Combine the sour cream, yogurt, mustard, and vinegar. Add pepper.

3. Pour dressing over the vegetables. Chill for an hour to blend flavors.

Low Sodium Asian Beef Salad

This beef salad is a tasty alternative to Asian-style beef salads that are loaded with sodium due to the soy sauce in them.

Prep Time: 15 m

Serves: 2

Nutritional Info: Calories: 947, Sodium: 1137 mg, Dietary Fiber: 6.2 g, Total Fat: 83.7 g, Total Carbs: 17.4 g, Protein: 40.2 g

INGREDIENTS

....

NOODLES

2 small-medium heads of iceberg lettuce, spiralized

MAIN INGREDIENTS

½ pound rare roast beef, cut into strips

1 basket grape tomatoes, washed and drained

1 small red onion, thinly sliced

1 large package pre-washed spinach leaves, shredded

2 Tbsp. prepared horseradish (without soy oil or sugar)

¾ cup olive oil

....

DIRECTIONS

1. Spiralize the iceberg lettuce into flat crescents.

2. Combine the beef, the tomatoes, noodles and the shredded spinach.

3. Mix the horseradish and the olive oil and pour over the other ingredients.

4. Toss to mix salad.

5. Serve chilled.

Note: Use any combination of greens you like—romaine is always a good choice and if you must restrict your intake of Vitamin K because you take blood thinners, a good alternative to spinach. Pour dressing over the vegetables. Chill for an hour to blend flavors.

MEDITERRANEAN PASTA SALAD

GF | P

This is more of a pasta side dish than a salad. If you want the INGREDIENTS to "stick together" more, you can replace 2 Tbsp. of the olive oil with mayonnaise or Greek yogurt—it just won't be Paleo any more.

Prep Time: 12 m

Serves: 4

Calories: 176, Sodium: 55 mg, Dietary Fiber: 1.0 g, Total Fat: 5.8 g, Total Carbs: 17.8 g, Protein: 14.0 g

INGREDIENTS

....

4 cups courgette, spiralized

2 cups cooked chicken breast, cut in bite-sized pieces

3 hard-boiled egg whites, diced

1 small red onion, diced

2 garlic cloves, minced

3 Tbsp. olive oil

Juice of ½ lemon

1 tsp. basil

½ tsp. dried rosemary

Sliced black olives (for garnish)

....

DIRECTIONS

1. Spiralize the courgette into thin strands.

2. Blanche the noodles if you desire a softer noodle. Otherwise leave raw.

3. Combine the noodles, chicken, diced egg whites, and red onion in a small bowl.

4. Combine the other ingredients and whisk to blend well. Pour over the noodle/chicken mixture and toss to blend.

5. Garnish with sliced olives if desired.

Note: Can also garnish with some crumbled feta cheese if not Paleo.

MEXICAN SLAW

GF | P | WL | V | VG

This variation on a theme salad pairs cabbage with radishes and green chillies. If you like more heat, use substitute a hotter pepper like a jalapeno or serrano.

Prep Time: 10 m

Serves: 4–6

Calories: 75, Sodium: 35 mg, Dietary Fiber: 1.6 g, Total Fat: 3.4 g, Total Carbs: 10.3 g, Protein: 1.1 g

INGREDIENTS

....

1/2 small head green cabbage, spiralized

1/2 small head Cabbage, spiralized

1 small bunch red radishes

2 fresh green chillies (or Hatch chiles)

Juice of three limes

1 Tbsp. rapeseed oil

1 bunch fresh coriander, minced (about 2 cups)

¼ tsp. Cayenne pepper

....

DIRECTIONS

1. Remove tough outer leaves from cabbage and cut out core. Spiralize the cabbage.

2. Trim the radishes and slice thinly.

3. De-seed the peppers and cut into small dice.

4. Mix the cabbages, radishes, and peppers in a large bowl and set aside.

5. Mix together the lime juice and pepper. Add the coriander and let sit for 5 minutes. Whisk in the soil. Pour vinaigrette over the vegetables and toss to blend. Either serve immediately, or chill for an hour.

NOODLES & HUMMUS SALAD

GF

This cross-cultural dish—originally made with Soba noodles—is a fresh take on pasta salad that's perfect for a light lunch or as a dinner side.

Prep Time: 10 m

Serves: 4

Calories: 454, Sodium: 1107 mg, Dietary Fiber: 5.7 g, Total Fat: 213 g, Total Carbs: 54.6 g, Protein: 11.4 g

INGREDIENTS

....

4 cups courgette, spiralized

2 medium carrots, spiralized

¾ cup prepared hummus (classic, not flavored)

1 bell pepper, seeded and diced

3 spring onions, thinly sliced

¼ cup rapeseed oil

1 tsp. dark sesame oil

4 Tbsp. soy sauce

4 Tbsp. rice vinegar

1 tsp. ginger

2 Tbsp. fresh mint

1 tsp. crushed red pepper flakes

....

DIRECTIONS

1. Spiralize the courgette and carrots into thick strands.

2. Blanche the carrot noodles. If you like soft courgette noodles, then blanche the courgette, otherwise leave uncooked.

3. Combine the noodles with the peppers, and spring onions in a large bowl.

4. Combine the oil, vinegar, herbs, and spices. Mix well and pour over the noodle/vegetable combination.

5. Stir in the hummus and toss to blend.

POTATO-VEGGIE LATKES

Chances are you love latkes (who doesn't?) but hardly ever make them because it's so time-consuming to grate the potatoes and other vegetables. With a Paderno or Veggetti, that's in the past and there will be a lot more latkes in your future.

Prep Time: 20 m

Serves: 6

Nutritional Info: Calories: 214, Sodium: 80 mg, Dietary Fiber: 3.6 g, Total Fat: 4.0 g, Total Carbs: 40.5 g, Protein: 6.4 g

INGREDIENTS

....

4 large baking potatoes, spiralized

1 large carrot, spiralized

1 large yellow onion, grated

2 eggs, beaten

3 Tbsp. matzo meal (or Panko breadcrumbs)

Dash kosher salt

Dash black pepper

Vegetable oil for frying

....

DIRECTIONS

1. Spiralize the carrot and potatoes (scrubbed and peeled) into flat crescents.

2. Combine in with the grated onion in a colander set over a large bowl. Press down with the back of a spoon to squeeze as much moisture as possible out of the mixture.

3. Let drain for five minutes.

4. Discard the liquid, then combine the vegetables with the eggs and matzo meal.

5. Add ground pepper and salt.

6. Coat the bottom of a heavy-duty frying pan (cast-iron is perfect) with oil.

7. Drop spoonfuls of the batter into the oil and flatten with the back of a spoon or spatula.

8. Fry the latkes until they are golden brown on one side, then flip them over to brown on the other side.

9. Drain on a baking sheet that's been lined with paper towels.

10. Serve hot with sour cream and apple sauce.

Note: *If you are trying to limit your intake of simple carbs, it's easy to make these vegetable fritters out of quality-carb veggies like courgette and other squash instead of potatoes.*

Colorful Carrot & Beet Slaw

GF | P | V | VG

This colorful slaw substitutes beetroot and carrots for the more common cabbage and uses a basic vinaigrette as the dressing instead of mayonnaise.

Prep Time: 15 m

Serves: 4

Calories: 161, Sodium: 197 mg, Dietary Fiber: 3.7 g, Total Fat: 11.0 g, Total Carbs: 15.4 g, Protein: 2.2 g

INGREDIENTS

....

3 large beetroot, spiralized

4 large carrots, spiralized

2 Tbsp. Dijon mustard

3 Tbsp. red wine vinegar

3 Tbsp. olive oil

1 tsp. black pepper

....

DIRECTIONS

1. Spiralize the beetroot and carrots (thin strands recommended) and place into a plate.

2. Combine oil, vinegar, mustard, and pepper. Pour vinaigrette over noodles. Garnish with parsley.

SHAVED ASPARAGUS, YELLOW SQUASH, AND MINT SALAD

The fresh taste of uncooked asparagus makes this salad bright, light, and tangy. The addition of the lemon juice keeps the acidity high, without being too sharp. This is an excellent accompaniment to fish or shellfish.

Servings: 4

Prep time: 10 minutes

Cooking time: 10 minutes

Nutritional Info: Calories: 197, Sodium: 34 mg. Dietary fiber: 2.7 g. Total fat: 14.9 g. Total carbs: 7.3 g. Protein: 3.4 g.

INGREDIENTS

....

2 large yellow squash, spiralized

4 asparagus

1 handful toasted, crushed hazelnuts

1 Tbsp. chopped mint

3 Tbsp. lemon juice

2 Tbsp. sherry or white wine vinegar

1 tsp. honey

3 Tbsp. extra virgin olive oil

Parmesan or pecorino cheese shavings

....

DIRECTIONS

DRESSING

1. In a medium sized bowl, whisk together lemon juice, vinegar, honey, and olive oil. Set aside

SALAD

1. Spiralize yellow squash into thin rings.

2. Heat a pot of lightly salted water to boiling.

3. Add squash rings and blanche till just tender, but still al dente about 2-3 minutes.

4. Drain well, and allow to cool fully.

5. Using a vegetable peeler, shave the asparagus very thinly lengthwise. Shavings should be very thin.

6. Toss asparagus, cooled squash rings, dressing, mint, and hazelnuts together.

7. Add salt and pepper to taste.

8. Serve with shaved cheese over the top.

THAI CHICKEN & NOODLE SALAD

A wonderful variation on Asian Chicken & Noodle Salad, this recipe includes nutty flavors and a little bit of heat. Since peanuts and peanut butter are off the menu for GF diets, consider making this with almond butter for a change.

Prep Time: 1 h 20 m

Serves: 4

Calories: 551, Sodium: 1,523 mg, Dietary Fiber: 6.2 g, Total Fat: 19.9 g, Total Carbs: 55 g, Protein: 39.8 g

INGREDIENTS

....

3 cups courgette or yellow squash, spiralized

2 medium carrots, spiralized

2 cups cooked chicken breast cut in bite-size pieces

½ cup creamy peanut butter

3 Tbsp. water

4 Tbsp. gluten-free soy sauce

3 Tbsp. rice vinegar

2 Tbsp. chili-garlic sauce

2 Tbsp. fresh ginger, grated

1 Tbsp. light brown sugar

1 small bunch coriander, leaves only chopped

1 bunch spring onions, sliced thin

1 bell pepper, cut in thin slices

....

DIRECTIONS

1. Slit the courgette, squash and carrots along one side and spiralize into thin rings. Blanche the resulting noodles if you desire a softer noodle. Otherwise leave raw.

2. In a large serving bowl, combine the noodles, chicken, grated carrots, bell pepper, coriander, and spring onions.

3. In a food processor or blender, combine the peanut butter, soy sauce, chili-garlic sauce, brown sugar, and water. Blend until smooth. If the dressing is too thick, add a little more water.

4. Pour dressing over salad and toss to coat.

5. Serve chilled or at room temperature.

THAI CHICKEN SALAD

This spicy salad is served cold but will warm you up. It can also be made with strips of rare beef or juicy pork.

Prep Time: 15 m

Serves: 2–4

Calories: 177, Sodium: 399 mg, Dietary Fiber: 5.9 g, Total Fat: 9.6 g, Total Carbs: 18.1 g, Protein: 10.8 g

INGREDIENTS

....

"PASTA"

2 large courgettes, spiralized

CHICKEN

½ rotisserie chicken, shredded

1 head Napa or Chinese cabbage, shredded

¼ cup fresh coriander chopped

1 cucumber, cut into matchsticks

¼ cup peanuts, chopped

3 spring onions, thinly sliced

DRESSING

1 garlic clove, minced

2 Tbsp. peanut butter

¼ tsp. sesame oil

2 Tbsp. water

½ Tbsp. lime juice

½ red chili pepper, deseeded and diced

¼ tsp. fish sauce

1 Tbsp. gluten-free tamari or soy sauce or substitute

....

DIRECTIONS

1. Spiralize the courgettes into thin strands. Heat or cook to your preferences.

2. Whisk dressing ingredients together in a small bowl. Don't be afraid to taste it before you're finished mixing, as you may want to increase or decrease certain ingredients to your taste. Add water to thin the dressing.

3. Mix all the salad ingredients in a large bowl and when it's complete, pour the dressing over the salad.

THAI GREEN PAPAYA SALAD

GF | WL | P

This traditional Thai salad is a refreshing blend of sweet and hot, with a salty accent of fish sauce. Note: substitute almonds for the peanuts to convert this to a Paleo recipe.

Prep Time: 20–25 m

Serves: 4

Calories: 451, Sodium: 785 mg, Dietary Fiber: 6.2 g, Total Fat: 17.1 g, Total Carbs: 69.5 g, Protein: 12.2 g

INGREDIENTS

....

2 green papayas, peeled

2 medium carrots, spiralized

2 cups bean sprouts

10 grape tomatoes, cut in half

½ cup fresh basil, chopped roughly

½ cup unsalted peanuts, chopped coarsely

2 Tbsp. rapeseed oil

½ tsp. soy sauce

2 Tbsp. fish sauce

Juice of two limes

....

DIRECTIONS

1. Spiralize the papaya and carrots into thin strands. Then mix with tomatoes and chopped basil.

2. Combine the oil, soy sauce, fish sauce, and lime juice. Pour the dressing over the salad and toss to combine.

3. Garnish with chopped peanuts.

COURGETTE PASTA ALA CHECCA

This no-cook variation of an Italian classic is gluten-free, vegan/vegetarian, low-cholesterol, low calorie, and kid-friendly.

Prep Time: 15 m

Serves: 2

Nutritional Info: Calories: 340, Sodium: 340, Dietary Fiber: 7.9 g, Total Fat: 13.4 g, Total Carbs: 26.6 g, Protein: 28.9 g

INGREDIENTS

....

"PASTA"

4 large courgette, spiralized

SAUCE

6 large ripe Tomatoes, diced

6-8 fresh basil leaves roughly chopped

4 spring onions, diced (white parts only)

2 large garlic cloves, minced

1 Tbsp. grated Parmesan cheese

¼ cup olive oil

Freshly ground pepper

....

DIRECTIONS

1. Combine all the ingredients except the courgette in a glass or ceramic bowl. Cover and allow to stand at room temperature for two hours to blend flavors. (Refrigerate if you won't use it right away, just bring the mixture to room temperature before mixing with the warm spiralized courgette)

2. Make thin strands out of courgette with your spiralizer.

3. Warm the strands by quickly dunking them in a pot of boiling water.

4. Drain pasta and top with room-temperature sauce.

5. Toss to distribute the sauce evenly throughout the pasta.

6. Serve immediately.

Note: Parmesan cheese is extremely salty, but 1 tablespoon divided among two servings is not a lot, especially if you don't add any additional salt. The trick to staying on any kind of eating plan is making the food palatable.

COURGETTE, SQUASH, AND APPLE SALAD WITH HAZELNUTS AND CRANBERRIES

A delicious, simple side salad, this recipe mixes the bold tastes of squash and courgette with the sweetness of apples and cranberries. Roasted almonds can be substituted for hazelnuts. Either way, the blend of flavors is a perfect mix of savory, sweet, and nutty.

Servings: 4

Prep time: 15 minutes

Cooking time: 30 minutes

Nutritional Info: Calories: 231, Sodium: 36 mg. Dietary fiber: 7.1 g. Total fat: 15.4 g. Total carbs: 22.0 g. Protein: 6.2 g.

INGREDIENTS

....

2 large courgettes, spiralized

2 large yellow squashes, spiralized

1 apple (gala or fuji recommended), spiralized

1 Tbsp. olive oil

1 small onion, diced finely

1 cup hazelnuts, toasted, skinned, and chopped

1 bunch spring onions, chopped (green parts only)

½ cup cranberries, chopped finely

1 bunch flat-leaf parsley, finely chopped

1 large lemon, juiced

....

DIRECTIONS

1. Preheat oven to 325

2. Spread hazelnuts in a single layer on a baking tray, and roast for 7-10 minutes

3. Let cool completely

4. When cooled, remove skins and chop coarsely.

5. Boil a large pot of lightly salted water.

6. Spiralize courgette and squash, into thin strands.

7. Add courgette and squash and cook until just tender and al dente, about 3-5 minutes.

8. Drain well, and set aside to cool.

9. Spiralize apple into thick strands.

10. Toss apple with lemon juice to prevent browning, and add flavor, then set aside.

11. Heat a heavy bottomed frying pan with 1 tablespoon oil. Add chopped onion and celery, and cook till softened, approximately 5-8 minutes. Do not let them brown, just wilt and soften.

12. Add salt and pepper to taste.

13. Set aside.

14. Add cranberries, spring onions, and parsley to the cooked celery and onions.

15. Add vegetable strands, hazelnuts, and apple.

16. Drizzle with remaining oil, and toss well.

17. Add salt, pepper, and additional lemon juice to taste.

18. Refrigerate for at least 20 minutes prior to serving.

19. Serve cool or cold.

SOUTHWESTERN SPICED SWEET POTATO AND BEET SPIRALS WITH CHILI-CORIANDER SOUR CREAM

A tasty and healthy snack, these baked vegetable spirals have just enough heat. Leaving the skins on the potatoes adds to the nutrition value of the dish. Be sure to check frequently while baking so as not to burn your spirals!

Servings: 4

Prep time: 10 minutes

Cooking time: 20 minutes

Nutritional Info: Calories: 448, Sodium: 1,555 mg. Dietary fiber: 5.0 g. Total fat: 25.1 g. Total carbs: 48 g. Protein: 10.5 g.

INGREDIENTS

....

POTATO AND BEET SPIRALS:

2 large sweet potatoes, spiralized

2 large beetroot, peeled & spiralized

1 large russet potato, spiralized

3 Tbsp. olive oil

2 tsp. salt

1 ½ tsp. ground cumin

1 ½ tsp. chile powder

107

1 ½ tsp. paprika

1 ½ tsp. ground black pepper

½-1 tsp. cayenne, to taste

CHILI-CORIANDER SOUR CREAM

1 cup sour cream

1 Tbsp. lime juice

2 tsp. sweet chili sauce

1 small garlic clove, minced or crushed

½ tsp. salt

½ tsp. black pepper

1 heaping Tbsp. coriander

....

DIRECTIONS

POTATO SPIRALS

1. Preheat oven to 425

2. Spiralize potato, sweet potatoes, and beetroot, into flat rings.

3. Combine salt, cumin, chile powder, paprika, pepper, and cayenne.

4. Toss spices and cut potatoes and beetroot together, till well coated.

5. Arrange all vegetables on a high-sided baking tray, in a single layer.

6. Bake on the middle rack of the oven, until bottom is browned, about 8-10 minutes.

7. Turn potatoes and beetroot over, and bake an additional 5-8 minutes.

8. Remove from oven and serve with chili-coriander sour cream.

CHILI-CORIANDER SOUR CREAM

1. Stir together all ingredients but coriander, and mix very well.

2. Lightly stir in coriander.

COURGETTE AND SQUASH SUMMER SALAD WITH GOLDEN RAISINS, PISTACHIOS, AND MINT

A delicious summery salad that pairs well with chicken. The vegetable stock adds a dimension to the noodles that plain water cannot, while adding no fat to the dish. Excellent for serving to vegetarians, there's no need for meat to make this dish delicious, but if you want to serve it as a main course, try topping with a grilled chicken breast.

Servings: 4

Prep time: 15 minutes

Cooking time: 20 minutes

Calories: 139, Sodium: 32 mg, Dietary Fiber: 3.8, Total Fat: 4.0 g, Total Carbs: 25.7 g, Protein: 4.7 g

INGREDIENTS:

....

1 large yellow squash, spiralized

1 large courgette, spiralized

1 Tbsp. lemon zest

Juice of 1 lemon

1/2 Tsp. honey

3 garlic cloves, crushed

1 1/4 cup vegetable stock

1 medium shallot, finely chopped

1/2 cup golden raisins

1/4 cup pistachios, chopped

2 Tbsp. fresh mint, chopped

Salt and pepper to taste

....

DIRECTIONS:

NOODLES:

1. Spiralize the yellow squash and courgette.

2. Bring the vegetable stock to a boil.

3. Add spiralized vegetables. Boil for 1-2 minutes until just tender.

4. Drain reserving the broth. Set aside to cool.

DRESSING:

1. Whisk together lemon zest, lemon juice, honey, and 1/4 cup reserved broth.

2. Add garlic cloves and set aside for at least 30 minutes.

3. Assembling the dish:

4. Heat a large skillet to medium heat.

5. Add shallots, raisins, pistachios and 1/2 - 1 Tsp. salt.

6. Toss well and cook 1-2 minutes till lightly toasted. If mixture sticks to pan, add 1-2 Tsp. reserved broth.

7. Add cooked noodles, and cook 2-3 more minutes till slightly crispy and golden.

8. Remove the garlic cloves from the dressing.

9. Toss dressing with noodle mixture.

10. Sprinkle with chopped mint.

11. Serve at room temperature.

SIDES

Think about your most memorable meals—often it wasn't the entrees that had you salivating, it was the dishes on the side. Why not make some memories with these recipes?

GF - Gluten-free

P - Paleo

WL - Weight-Loss

V - Vegetarian

Vg – Vegan

BLEU CHEESE & SPINACH PASTA

This is another chameleon of a dish that can do double-duty as a side or a salad, depending on the number of diners.

Prep Time: 25 m

Serves: 6

Calories: 153, Sodium: 411 mg, Dietary Fiber: 1.1 g, Total Fat: 12.7 g, Total Carbs: 4.1 g, Protein: 6.1 g

INGREDIENTS

....

3 cups courgette or yellow squash, spiralized

4 oz. bleu cheese, crumbled

1 large bunch spinach, chopped coarsely

1 small red onion, sliced into rings

1 cup vegetable broth

2 Tbsp. balsamic vinegar (may substitute red wine vinegar)

3 Tbsp. olive oil

½ tsp. black pepper

....

DIRECTIONS

1. Using a large frying pan, heat the onions in 1 Tbsp. oil until they are beginning to brown.

2. Combine the broth, the vinegar, the black pepper and the chopped spinach and add to the pan. Cook for 3 minutes until the spinach has wilted.

3. While cooking broth, spiralize courgette or squash into thin strands.

4. Add the noodles and the cheese to the broth, stir to combine and cook until the cheese is melted, about 5 minutes.

MEDITERRANEAN SQUASH STIR-FRY

This side dish can be customized in multiple ways. Slice the squash and tomatoes into rounds for a pleasing presentation, substitute green tomatoes for a tangy variation.

Prep Time: 10 m

Serves: 2

Nutritional Info: Calories: 331, Sodium: 95 mg, Dietary Fiber: 12.0 g, Total Fat: 17.9 g, Total Carbs: 40.6 g, Protein: 11.8 g

INGREDIENTS

....

"PASTA"

3 large courgette, spiralized

2 large yellow squash

MAIN INGREDIENTS

1 large yellow onion

2 ripe tomatoes, diced or cut into rounds

2 large garlic cloves, minced

1 Tbsp. Italian seasoning

2 Tbsp. Olive oil

4 Tbsp. water (as needed)

Parmesan cheese

....

DIRECTIONS

1. Spiralize the courgette and yellow squash into thick strands.

2. Put the oil and 2 Tbsp. of water in a medium frying pan.

3. Combine the "pasta" and MAIN ingredients in the frying pan and cook on medium until the vegetables are soft but not mushy.

4. Sprinkle with the Italian seasoning and cook another minute or so to blend the flavors.

5. If necessary, add another tablespoon or two of water.

6. Sprinkle with parmesan cheese and serve immediately or at room temperature.

Noodle Kugel

GF

Is it a side dish or a dessert? Depends on the occasion and the amount of sugar added.

Prep Time: 80 m

Serves: 8–10

Calories: 199, Sodium: 166 mg, Dietary Fiber: __, Total Fat: 11.6 g, Total Carbs: 16.9 g, Protein: 7.8 g

INGREDIENTS

....

2 cups courgette, spiralized

1 8-oz. container cottage cheese

1 8-oz. container sour cream

1 ½ cups milk

½ oz butter, melted

2 eggs

¼ cup granulated sugar

....

DIRECTIONS

1. Preheat oven to 350 degrees.

2. In a large mixing bowl, combine the cottage cheese, sour cream, butter, eggs, sugar, and milk.

3. Add the spiralized courgette (thick strands recommended) and mix well.

4. Coat a glass baking pan (approx 13 x 9) with butter or non-stick spray and fill with the noodle mixture.

5. Bake for an hour at 375 until browned on top.

Note: To make a sweeter dessert kugel, increase the sugar to 2/3 cup and add 1 tsp. vanilla extract.

Pasta Salad — Italian Style

This is a perfect side dish to bring to a barbecue or serve as a summery side. Even hard-core carbohydrate addicts will chow down on the salad. Substitute cubes of deli ham for the salami if worried about sodium intake.

Prep Time: 20 m

Serves: 4

Calories: 266, Sodium: 466 mg, Dietary Fiber: 3.2 g, Total Fat: 22.4 g, Total Carbs: 11.5 g, Protein: 9.0 g

INGREDIENTS

....

"PASTA"

2 large courgettes, spiralized

1 large carrot, spiralized

SALAD

¼ cup cherry tomatoes, halved

¼ cup basil, chopped

½ red pepper, diced

2 spring onions, chopped

¼ lb. deli salami, cubed

DRESSING

1/3 cup olive oil

¼ cup grated Parmesan cheese (not fresh)

3 Tbsp. lemon juice

1 ½ tsp. dried oregano

2 garlic cloves, minced

½-¼ tsp. salt

¼ tsp. pepper

....

DIRECTIONS

1. Spiralize the courgettes and carrot into thin strands. Heat or cook to your preference or leave raw.

2. Combine "pasta" with the salad vegetables.

3. Combine the salad dressing ingredients, whisking with a fork.

4. Pour salad dressing over pasta salad and mix well.

5. Refrigerate for up to three hours before serving.

PERFUMED NOODLES WITH FRUIT & NUTS

This is a gold-toned adaptation of the classic Middle Eastern dish "jeweled rice." Add cooked chicken or lamb to transform it from a side dish into an entrée.

Prep Time: 20 m

Serves: 4–6

Nutritional Info: Calories: 418, Sodium: 418 mg, Dietary Fiber: 6.3 g, Total Fat: 30.0 g, Total Carbs: 38.9 g, Protein: 4.9 g

INGREDIENTS

....

4 cups squash, spiralized

2/3 cup dried chopped dried apricots

1/3 cup golden raisins

½ cup dried cherries (or cranberries)

½ cup coconut oil

1 tsp. ground cardamom

1 thread saffron (if desired)

2/3 cup pistachio nuts, shelled and chopped

¼ tsp. ground pepper

....

DIRECTIONS

1. Lightly sauté the chopped nuts in a tablespoon of the coconut oil.

2. Add the fruit and spices.

3. Add the remaining coconut oil and the spiralized squash (thin strands recommended).

4. Sauté lightly until all the flavors blend.

5. Serve immediately.

Note: You can substitute dried pears for the apricots; the result won't be as authentic, but pears pair well with cardamom.

SESAME NOODLES

GF | VG | V

This is comfort food with an Asian accent. Make sure to buy a brand of almond butter made without added salt or sugar.

Prep Time: 10 m

Serves: 1

Calories: 382, Sodium: 186 mg, Dietary Fiber: 9.7 g, Total Fat: 28.9 g, Total Carbs: 29.8 g, Protein: 14.1 g

INGREDIENTS

....

"PASTA"

4 medium sized courgette, spiralized

SAUCE

1/3 cup creamy almond butter

1 Tbsp. dark sesame oil

1 Tbsp. honey

2 spring onions, sliced for garnish

....

DIRECTIONS

1. Spiralize the four courgettes into thick crescents. Set aside in a medium-sized serving bowl. This is meant to be a cold dish, but you can warm the noodles if you like.

2. Combine almond butter, sesame oil and honey in a glass measuring cup.

3. Mix noodles with sauce and serve.

SQUASH SAUTE

GF | WL | V

Mix and match yellow squash and courgette for a more colorful dish.

Prep Time: 25–30 m

Serves: 8

Calories: 100, Sodium: 39 mg, Dietary Fiber: 2.2 g, Total Fat: 6.9 g, Total Carbs: 8.5 g, Protein: 2.9 g

INGREDIENTS

....

2 lbs. yellow squash, spiralized

1 lb. ripe Tomatoes, thinly sliced

1 medium yellow onion, thinly sliced

3 Tbsp. olive oil

2 large garlic cloves, minced

½ tsp. crushed dried red pepper flakes

1 Tbsp. Italian seasoning

Parmesan cheese for garnish

....

DIRECTIONS

1. Heat the oil in a large frying pan. Sauté the onion and garlic until the onion is translucent.

2. Add the tomatoes and sauté until the tomatoes have released their juices.

3. Spiralize the squash into thin crescents and sauté for 1-2 minutes.

4. Stir in the Italian seasoning and the pepper flakes.

5. Serve hot.

6. Garnish with parmesan cheese if desired.

Suspiciously Delicious Cabbage and Apples

A wonderful winter side dish, combining the sweetness of apples with the tart bitterness of cabbage. The cream mellows the tastes, and gives it a rich flavor. It is excellent served beside pork.

Servings: 4-6

Prep time: 15 minutes

Cooking time: 30 minutes

Nutritional Info: Calories: 160, Sodium: 37 mg. Dietary fiber: 3.6 g. Total fat: 0.0 g. Total carbs: 19.4 g. Protein: 1.1 g.

Ingredients

....

3 large green apples (granny smith or other tart type), peeled and spiralized

1 medium green cabbage, cored and thinly sliced

1 medium yellow onion, finely chopped

2 garlic cloves, minced

1 Tbsp. fresh grated ginger

2 Tbsp. butter

¾ cup double cream

Salt and pepper to taste

....

DIRECTIONS

1. In a large frying pan, heat the butter until melted and starting to bubble.

2. Add onion and garlic and cook until softened, about 5 minutes.

3. Stir in the ginger, and cook for 1-2 more minutes, until fragrant.

4. Add cabbage and toss till well coated. Cook on medium heat for 15-20 minutes until cabbage is softened and slightly caramelized.

5. Turn heat to low, stir in cream, and scrape bottom and sides of pan well.

6. Cover, and cook on low for 10 minutes.

7. Uncover, add salt and pepper to taste.

8. Spiralize the apples into thin strands. Add apple noodles to the cabbage mixture, stirring to coat the apple thoroughly.

9. Cook 2-5 more minutes to let some liquid evaporate.

10. Serve hot.

VEGGIE PASTA WITH BACON AND SWISS CHARD

GF

This rustic combination of pasta, bacon and greens is a mainstay of Mediterranean cooking.

Prep Time: 25–30 m

Serves: 4

Calories: 616, Sodium: 2,116 mg, Dietary Fiber: 2.5 g, Total Fat: 47.7 g, Total Carbs: 10.3 g, Protein: 35.9 g

INGREDIENTS

....

4 cups courgette or yellow squash, spiralized

¾ pound bacon, cut into ½-inch slices

1 large yellow onion, sliced thinly

2 large bunches Swiss chard, chopped

3 Tbsp. olive oil

2 Tbsp. balsamic vinegar

¾ cup grated Parmesan cheese

....

DIRECTIONS

1. Spiralize the courgettes (thick strands recommended). Blanche the noodles and reserve 1 cup of pasta-cooking liquid. Place the cooked pasta in a large serving bowl.

2. Fry the bacon in a large, heavy frying pan until it is beginning to crisp (about 10 minutes). Remove bacon from pan and drain on paper towels.

3. Remove all but 3 tablespoons of bacon fat from frying pan.

4. Add onion and sauté over medium heat until soft and translucent. Add the chard and the reserved pasta-cooking liquid.

5. Stir to combine and cook until the chard is wilted.

6. Pour over the pasta.

7. Crumble the bacon and sprinkle over the pasta.

8. Garnish with the cheese.

Note: Eliminate the Parmesan cheese to make this dish Paleo-friendly as well as vegan.

COURGETTE AND POTATO PANCAKES

Fried and crispy, the addition of courgette to these unique potato pancakes makes them a healthy and delicious choice of a side dish. Remember to drain the courgette well before tossing it with the egg, for better cohesion of the pancake.

Servings: 2

Prep time: 10 minutes

Cooking time: 25 minutes

Nutritional Info: Calories: 358, Sodium: 121 mg. Dietary fiber: 9.2 g. Total fat: 15.7 g. Total carbs: 16.6 g. Protein: 13.6 g.

INGREDIENTS

....

2 large courgettes, spiralized

1 large potato, peeled & spiralized

1 egg

1 Tbsp. chopped parsley

1 tsp. lemon zest

1-2 tsp. almond flour

1 Tbsp. unsalted butter

Sour cream or greek yogurt to accompany

Salt and pepper to taste

....

DIRECTIONS

1. Spiralize both courgette and potatoes into thick rings.

2. Let stand in a colander for at least 30 minutes to drain. The better drained they are, the better the pancakes will stick together.

3. In a bowl, beat egg, parsley, and lemon zest. Add a pinch of salt and pepper and beat well.

4. Take courgette and potato mixture out of colander, and roll in paper towels. Squeeze well to drain all residual moisture.

5. Add 1-2 teaspoon almond flour to soak up the last of the moisture.

6. Mix courgette and potato mixture with egg mixture and toss well to coat.

7. Turn oven to warm, to keep cooked pancakes hot while frying.

8. Heat frying pan on medium-high heat and melt butter in it.

9. Drop a spoonful of courgette-potato pancake mixture into pan, and press flat with spatula. Cook approximately 3-4 minutes, till crispy, flip and repeat on other side.

10. Put cooked pancakes on covered plate in over till ready to serve.

11. Serve with greek yogurt or sour cream.

ENTREES

The entrée is the main course, the base a meal is built upon. If you take away all the extras, what you're left with is the entrée.

GF - Gluten-free

P - Paleo

WL - Weight-Loss

V - Vegetarian

Vg – Vegan

BEEF PAPRIKASH WITH SQUASH NOODLES

Also known as "beef goulash," this recipe is often made with the addition of sour cream, but the real heart of the flavor is the interaction of meat and paprika, and this version of a comfort food classic (served on a bed of squash noodles) is totally Paleo-friendly.

Prep Time: 3 h

Serves: 2

Nutritional Info: Calories: 572, Sodium: 817 mg, Dietary Fiber: 17.7 g, Total Fat: 25.4 g, Total Carbs: 53.0 g, Protein: 40.7 g

INGREDIENTS

....

NOODLES

4 cups yellow squash, spiralized

PAPRIKASH

½ lb. stewing steak, cut into cubes

2 cups beef broth

2 Tbsp. olive oil

8 Tomatoes, seeded and diced

2 large yellow onions, diced

1 green bell pepper, seeded and diced

2 cups beef broth

2 large garlic cloves, minced

3 Tbsp. paprika (or to taste)

2 tsp. caraway seeds

....

DIRECTIONS

1. Preheat oven to 350.

2. Sear the beef cubes in the olive oil in the bottom of a Dutch oven. Push the beef cubes to the side and Saute the onions, bell pepper, and garlic, cooking until the onions are translucent.

3. Add the tomatoes and beef stock.

4. Roast at 350 for 2-2 ½ hours until the beef is tender is so tender it can be shredded with a fork.

5. Spiralize the squash into thick strands. Place the noodles into boiling water for a couple minutes, just enough to warm them.

6. Serve the paprikash over warmed "noodles."

Note: *This can be made in a crockpot.*

BEEF RAGU OVER POTATO PASTA

Try this new combination of meat and potatoes as a change of pace. Substitute courgette pasta for the potatoes to make the recipe low carb.

Prep Time: 55 m

Serves: 4

Calories: 520, Sodium: 84 mg, Dietary Fiber: 7.7 g, Total Fat: 20.6 g, Total Carbs: 55.6 g, Protein: 23.7 g

INGREDIENTS

....

4 cups potato, spiralized

1 ½ pounds minced beef or turkey

1 large yellow onion, chopped coarsely

3 large garlic cloves, minced

1/3 cup dry red wine

2 14 oz cans "Italian style" diced tomato

1 large carrot, coarsely chopped

2 Tbsp. Italian seasoning

1/3 cup half and half

2 Tbsp. olive oil

Grated Parmesan cheese for garnish

....

DIRECTIONS

1. Heat oil in a large saucepan. Add the meat, onion, garlic, and carrot. Sauté until meat is no longer pink, about 8 minutes. Add wine and cook for 3-5 minutes until it evaporates, stirring constantly. Stir in the tomatoes (juice included) the half and half and the Italian seasoning.

2. Reduce heat, cover the pan and simmer until the sauce has thickened (about 25 minutes).

3. While simmering the ragu, spiralize the potato into thick strands. Cook as you prefer.

4. When the sauce is done, serve over the potato noodles.

5. If you're not following a Paleo diet, garnish with parmesan cheese if desired.

CARROT PASTA WITH MUSHROOM SAUCE

This dish is both colorful and hearty, and can do double-duty as a vegetarian entrée for one or as a show-stopping starter for two.

Prep Time: 15–20 m

Serves: 2

Calories: 122, Sodium: 155 mg, Dietary Fiber: 3.0 g, Total Fat: 7.1 g, Total Carbs: 14.2 g, Protein: 2.2 g

INGREDIENTS

....

"PASTA"

3 large carrots, spiralized

SAUCE

¾ cup chopped mushrooms, any kind

2 Tbsp. shallot, chopped (may substitute ¼ yellow onion, chopped)

3 tsp. olive oil

3/4 tsp. dried basil

2 large garlic cloves, minced

Pinch black pepper

Pinch salt

....

DIRECTIONS

1. Spiralize the carrots into thin strands. Set aside.

2. Add onion (or shallots) and garlic to heated oil in medium-size frying pan and sauté for 2-3 minutes.

3. Add the mushrooms to the pan and heat for 6-7 minutes or until the mushroom "liquid" has evaporated. Season with salt and pepper.

4. Add the carrot "pasta" and mix well. Cook for another 5-10 minutes until the pasta is the texture you prefer.

BEET PASTA WITH SALMON

Salmon and beetroot are the nutritional equivalent of Superman and Wonder Woman, so pairing them up is like having the Justice League converge on your plate! Combined with creamed cauliflower, this blending of flavors is truly something to savor.

Prep Time: 30 m

Serves: 2

Calories: 752, Sodium: 905 mg, Dietary Fiber: 13.2 g, Total Fat: 47.4 g, Total Carbs: 47.3 g, Protein: 44.3g

INGREDIENTS

....

"PASTA"

1lb o r 454 gms large beetroot, spiralized

SAUCE

2 6-oz. salmon fillets

1 Tbsp. coconut oil

1 medium onion, chopped

3 garlic cloves, minced

3 cups cauliflower florets

1/3 cup lemon juice

1 ½ Tbsp. lemon zest

142

1 cup canned coconut milk

1/2 tsp. salt

1/4 tsp. black pepper

1/2 tsp. paprika

1/2 tsp. mustard powder

1/2 tsp. garlic powder

1 tsp. cumin

....

DIRECTIONS

1. Pre-heat oven to 250°.

2. Remove the beet greens, and peel the beetroot. Spiralize the beetroot into thick strands. Boil for 20 minutes until soft, then set aside.

3. While boiling the beetroot, melt the coconut oil in a medium frying pan, then sauté the onion and garlic cloves for 4-6 minutes in coconut oil in a medium pan.

4. Steam cauliflower until tender (usually 5-7 minutes), then put in blender or food processor along with the garlic, onions, cumin, lemon juice and zest, coconut milk, pepper and salt. Process until smooth.

5. Line a cookie sheet with aluminium foil or coat with non-stick spray.

6. Mix the mustard powder, paprika, cumin, garlic powder, and salt and sprinkle it over the raw salmon.

7. Place the salmon on the treated cookie sheet and bake until the salmon is done (8-10 minutes, depending on thickness of the fillets).

8. Pour the spicy cauliflower sauce in a small saucepan and bring to a quick boil.

9. To serve, divide "pasta" onto two plates, cover with sauce and top with salmon pieces.

ASTONISHING BEEF STEW

A healthy and hearty winter meal, anchovies make this beef stew interesting and delicious. Make sure to brown the beef well, as crispy outsides will give it cohesion and add flavor. Also, remember to deglaze the pan that you brown the meat in. All those crispy bits taste amazing in the stew!

Servings: 8-10

Prep time: 20 minutes

Cooking time: 3 hours

Nutritional Info: Calories: 376, Sodium: 1760 mg. Dietary fiber: 5.9 g. Total fat: 20.6 g. Total carbs: 27.6 g. Protein: 16.2 g.

INGREDIENTS

....

1 large courgette, spiralized

1 large yellow squash, spiralized

5 - 5 ½ pounds stewing steak, cut into 2-3 inch pieces

⅓ cup mixed olive and rapeseed oil

2 leeks, washed and sliced thinly

1 large onion, diced

8 garlic cloves, minced or crushed

2 carrots, diced finely

4 celery stalks, diced finely

4 oz white mushrooms, roughly chopped

¼ cup tomato paste

2 anchovies

½ cup red wine vinegar

1 cup red wine

3 cups beef broth

1 cup canned whole tomatoes with juice

1 ½ tsp. salt

3 bay leaves

¾ tsp. dried thyme

⅓ cup chopped fresh parsley

Salt and pepper to taste

....

DIRECTIONS

1. Season the beef with salt and pepper, lightly.

2. In a large, heavy bottomed frying pan, heat several tablespoon of the mixed oil.

3. Brown the beef over high heat, adding more oil as needed. Remove, and set aside.

4. Lower heat, and add all vegetables except spiralized vegetables. Cook for 5-10 minutes, until softened.

5. Stir in tomato paste, and anchovies, and cook about 5 minutes to melt the tomato paste and anchovies, mixing well.

6. Add the beef back to the pan, and any juices that have drained. Add the wine, vinegar, and tomatoes with juice. Use a spatula or slotted spoon to break up the tomatoes. Bring to a boil.

7. Add the stock, enough to cover the vegetables and beef in the pot (this may require slightly more than 3 cups). Add the salt, bay and thyme, and bring to a boil.

8. Simmer, partially covered, about 2-3 hours.

9. Remove from heat and cool to room temperature, then put in the refrigerator. When fully cold, and fat has rendered to the top, skim off as much fat as possible.

10. Put back on low heat, and reheat slowly. Cook 20-30 minutes, on low, just simmering. Toward the end, mix in half the parsley.

11. While simmering the stew, spiralize both courgette and squash, into thick rings. Set aside.

12. Place spiralized squash in serving bowls, then pour hot beef stew over top. The heat from the stew will lightly cook the rings, creating a delicious contrast in textures and flavors.

13. Garnish with the remaining parsley and serve.

CHICKEN PARMESAN WITH NOODLES

This version of the Italian comfort food classic has lightened up but lost nothing in taste.

Prep Time: 60 m

Serves: 4

Calories: 661, Sodium: 546 mg, Dietary Fiber: 6.9 g, Total Fat: 41.7 g, Total Carbs: 24.5 g, Protein: 53.3 g

INGREDIENTS

....

"PASTA"

3 large courgettes, spiralized

CHICKEN PARMESAN

3 boneless chicken breasts

2 eggs, beaten

1 cup walnuts

½ cup dried Parmesan cheese

1 Tbsp. Italian seasoning

4-6 oz. tomato paste

8 oz. pizza sauce

½ cup mozzarella cheese, grated

2 Tbsp. olive oil

....

DIRECTIONS

1. Preheat oven to 350° F.

2. Spiralize the courgettes (thick strands recommended). Heat or cook as you prefer.

3. Chop 1 cup of walnuts in a food processor, then pour into a large bowl.

4. Combine Parmesan cheese, Italian seasoning, and pepper. Add to the chopped walnuts and mix well.

5. Cut chicken breasts in thirds. Dip them in the beaten egg, then into the walnut/cheese mix.

6. Add the olive oil to a large frying pan and brown the chicken pieces over medium heat.

7. Mix the pizza sauce with the tomato paste.

8. Arrange browned chicken pieces in a glass baking pan that's been treated with cooking spray. Pour the pizza sauce/tomato paste mixture on top of the chicken pieces.

9. Top the chicken and sauce with the Mozzarella cheese.

10. Bake at 350 for 25-30 minutes until the chicken is cooked through and the Mozzarella is melted and bubbly brown.

11. Serve the Parmesan chicken over the pasta.

CHICKEN PESTO PASTA

This meal is an "almost-homemade" entrée you can throw together in minutes.

Prep Time: 35 m

Serves: 4

Calories: 458, Sodium: 178 mg, Dietary Fiber: 5.0 g, Total Fat: 33.3 g, Total Carbs: 15.7 g, Protein: 26.9 g

INGREDIENTS

....

"PASTA"

2 large courgettes, spiralized

1 large carrot, spiralized

SAUCE

2 cups shredded, cooked chicken

2 garlic cloves, minced

1 Tbsp. grated ginger

2 Tbsp. white wine

½ yellow onion, sliced thinly

¼ cup toasted sliced almonds

2 Tbsp. olive oil

¼ cup pre-made pesto sauce

1 cup coconut milk

....

DIRECTIONS

1. Spiralize the courgettes into thin strands. Heat or cook to your preferences.

2. Heat the olive oil in a medium frying pan, then cook the garlic until it begins to brown. Remove and drain on paper towels.

3. Add the onion and ginger to the same still-hot frying pan and cook for 3-4 minutes, until the onion turns translucent.

4. Add the chicken pieces and sauté until they're lightly brown. (They're already cooked, so don't keep them on the heat too long.)

5. Combine the pesto, wine, and coconut milk and pour over the chicken.

6. Reduce heat and simmer for 10 minutes, stirring constantly.

7. Serve the sauce over the "pasta" and top with the fried garlic, sliced almonds, and fresh, chopped basil.

CHILI MAC

GF

This quick-fix dinner offers everyone's favorite variation on Mac 'n Cheese with an extra veggie boost.

Prep Time: 25 m

Serves: 4–6

Calories: 398, Sodium: 673 mg, Dietary Fiber: 1.9 g, Total Fat: 21.2 g, Total Carbs: 20.4 g, Protein: 33.6 g

INGREDIENTS

....

2 cups courgette or yellow squash, spiralized

1lb o r 454 gms ground turkey, turkey, or beef

1 large bell pepper, deseeded and diced

1 package taco seasoning mix

1 14.5-oz. can Mexican-style stewed tomatoes

½ cup water

2 cups shredded Cheddar Cheese (or use "Mexican blend)

....

DIRECTIONS

1. Preheat oven to 375.

2. In a large frying pan brown the meat, onion, and green pepper until the meat is cooked through.

3. Add the canned tomatoes (including the juice) the water, and the taco seasoning.

4. Simmer 5-10 minutes, stirring occasionally.

5. Spiralize the courgette or yellow squash to make noodles (flat rings recommended). Then combine the noodles with the meat/sauce mixture.

6. Coat a baking dish with butter or non-stick spray. Place half the noodles in the dish, add half the chili mixture, and to with half the cheese.

7. Add another layer of noodles, chili and cheese with the remaining ingredients.

8. Bake in the oven for 5 minutes, or until the cheese is melted.

9. Serve immediately.

CHICKEN, VEGGIE & PESTO PASTA

This hearty version of Pasta Primavera gets an extra dimension from the presence of pesto.

Prep Time: 40 m

Serves: 4

Calories: 511, Sodium: 314 mg, Dietary Fiber: 8.5 g, Total Fat: 23.1 g, Total Carbs: 23.1 g, Protein: 52.9 g

INGREDIENTS

....

"PASTA"

4 large courgettes, spiralized

SAUCE

4 boneless, skinless chicken breasts cut into 1-inch pieces

½ cup fresh Parmesan cheese, shredded

½ cup artichoke hearts, drained and quartered

6 oz asparagus, trimmed and cut into ½-inch pieces

2/3 cup peas, fresh or frozen

1 large garlic clove, chopped

4 spring onions, chopped

2 Tbsp. pine nuts

2 Tbsp. olive oil

1/3 cup white wine

1/8 tsp salt

½ tsp lemon juice

½ tsp lemon zest

2 Tbsp. water

1/4 tsp. black pepper

....

DIRECTIONS

1. Spiralize courgettes into thick strands.

2. Boil "pasta" for 4-6 minutes or until soft. Drain, reserving the liquid, and set aside in a warm place.

3. Combine the pine nuts, garlic, salt, and 1 tablespoon of oil in a food processor or blender and process until completely smooth.

4. Add the chopped parsley, water, Parmesan cheese, and lemon zest to the mixture. Process until completely combined.

5. Prepare the chicken:

6. Using a large frying pan, brown the chicken pieces in the remaining tablespoon of olive oil. This will take about 5 minutes over medium heat. Remove cooked meat from the pan and set it aside.

7. Add the onion to the frying pan and sauté over medium heat until the onion is translucent. Add the artichoke hearts and cook for another 3 minutes.

8. Add the wine to the vegetable mixture and cook for 2-3 minutes more, stirring occasionally.

9. Add the asparagus pieces and sauté until they are tender/crisp, about 2 minutes.

10. Stir in the "pasta," 1 ½ cups of the reserved pasta water, the pesto sauce, the chicken pieces, and the peas. Cook over medium heat until the peas are tender, about 2 minutes.

11. Remove from heat and stir in the lemon juice before serving.

Chinese Noodles & Chicken

This home-made version of a Chinese take-out favourite cuts back on the amount of sodium and sugar in the original dish. You can make it Paleo-friendly and Gluten-free by substituting soy sauce or substitute (available in most health food stores) for the soy sauce.

Prep Time: 20–25 m

Serves: 4

Calories: 288, Sodium: 625 mg, Dietary Fiber: 7.3 g, Total Fat: 6.6 g, Total Carbs: 37.1 g, Protein: 21.5 g

Ingredients

....

"PASTA"

2 large courgettes, spiralized

SAUCE

½ lb. boneless, skinless chicken, thinly sliced (thin slices)

5 cups Asian stir-fry vegetables, fresh or frozen

½ cup rice wine

1 Tbsp. soy sauce, preferably reduced sodium

2 tsp light brown sugar

4 tsp garlic-black bean sauce

1 ½ tsp cornflour

4 tsp peanut oil

1 tsp. fresh grated ginger

1 small yellow onion, finely sliced

½ cup water

....

DIRECTIONS

1. Spiralize the courgettes into thin strands. Heat or cook to your preferences.

2. Combine brown sugar, rice wine, garlic, black bean sauce, cornflour and soy sauce in a small bowl and set aside.

3. In a large frying pan, heat 2 teaspoon of peanut oil over medium heat. Add the ginger and onion. Sauté until the onions are translucent.

4. Add the Asian vegetables and ¼ cup of water and stir-fry for 3-4 minutes until crisply tender.

5. Combined cooked noodles with the sauce.

6. Add the rest of the peanut oil to the frying pan and sauté the chicken until thoroughly cooked.

7. Add the vegetables, sauce, and pasta to the pan, along with the remaining ¼ cup water.

8. Stir-fry for another 5 minutes until heated through.

CREAMY CHICKEN PASTA

This hearty dish is reminiscent of classic Hungarian goulashes. Use no-fat or low-fat sour cream to cut calories, or substitute Greek yogurt.

Prep Time: 15 m

Serves: 2

Calories: 775, Sodium: 1,582 mg, Dietary Fiber: 18.1 g, Total Fat: 35.9 g, Total Carbs: 18.1 g, Protein: 58.0 g

INGREDIENTS

....

"PASTA"

1 large courgette, spiralized

1 large carrot, spiralized

SAUCE

1 28-oz. can crushed tomatoes

1/3 cup sour cream

3 slices bacon, chopped

1 Tbsp. rapeseed oil

½ lb. boneless, skinless chicken breasts, cut in 1-inch pieces

1 medium green bell pepper, diced

1 medium yellow onion, chopped

1 Tbsp. all-purpose flour

2 garlic cloves, crushed

½ tsp. black pepper

....

DIRECTIONS

1. Spiralize the carrot and courgette into thin strands. Heat or cook to your preferences.

2. Heat oil in large frying pan over medium heat. Add onion and bacon, cooking for 2-4 minutes until bacon is cooked through.

3. Add bell pepper, garlic, chicken, and pepper. Sauté for another 5 minutes until the pepper and onion begin to soften.

4. Stir in flour to coat, then add the tomatoes and simmer for 4-6 minutes or until the chicken is thoroughly cooked and the sauce is bubbling up.

5. Remove from heat. Let sit for five minutes to cool slightly, then stir in sour cream.

6. Combine the sauce with the "pasta."

CREAMY PESTO COURGETTE LINGUINI WITH SHRIMP

A delicious, hearty alternative to traditional pastas, the courgette "linguini" lightens this dish, while not compromising on flavor. Remember to leave the "linguini" a little crunchy, they'll keep cooking while they drain!

Servings: 3-4

Prep time: 10 minutes

Cooking time: 10 minutes

Nutritional Info: Calories: 619, Sodium: 533 mg. Dietary fiber: 2.2 g. Total fat: 53.1 g. Total carbs: 11.4 g. Protein: 28.7 g.

INGREDIENTS

....

4-5 courgette, spiralized

½ cup unsalted butter

2 cup double cream

1/2 tsp. ground black pepper

1 cup grated Parmesan cheese

⅓ cup prepared pesto sauce

1lb o r 454 gms large shrimp, peeled and deveined

....

DIRECTIONS

1. Spiralize the courgettes linguini style (thick strands).

2. Bring a pot of lightly salted water to a gentle boil. Add courgette and blanche until just tender, about 2-3 minutes, drain and sprinkle a little olive oil on top.

3. For the sauce: melt butter over medium heat in large frying pan. With a whisk, stir in cream, then pepper. Cook for 6-8 minutes, stirring frequently.

4. Stir grated Parmesan cheese into sauce base, stirring well, until fully mixed.

5. Add the pesto sauce and stir well.

6. Cook for 3-5 minutes until just thickened.

7. Stir in shrimp. Cook until pink and well coated with sauce. About 5 minutes.

8. Serve over courgette linguini.

CURRIED CHICKEN WITH PASTA

The sweetness of the carrot "pasta" blends well with the curry spices in this recipe, but you can also use more strongly flavoured vegetable pasta like broccoli.

Prep Time: 25–30 m

Serves: 2–4

Calories: 629, Sodium: 351 mg, Dietary Fiber: 4.6 g, Total Fat: 25.0 g, Total Carbs: 30.1 g, Protein: 64.3 g

INGREDIENTS

....

"PASTA"

6 large carrots, spiralized

CHICKEN CURRY

4 boneless, skinless chicken breasts, cut into bite-sized pieces

1 16-oz. container plain yogurt

2 medium yellow onions, diced

2 large garlic cloves, minced

2 Tbsp. rapeseed oil

2 Tbsp. curry powder

1 tsp. cumin

1 tsp. turmeric

1 tsp. ginger

½ tsp. cayenne pepper

½ tsp. cinnamon

....

DIRECTIONS

1. Spiralize the carrots into thin strands. Heat or cook as you prefer.

2. Heat the oil in a large frying pan, then sauté the onions and garlic until translucent and fragrant.

3. Add the curry powder and other spices. Mix well until everything is golden yellow.

4. Add the chicken pieces to the spiced mixture and continue to cook until the chicken is white all the way through.

5. Turn the heat off. Wait five minutes and stir in the yogurt, mixing well. (Don't skip the waiting period or the yogurt will separate.)

6. Serve the chicken curry over the carrot pasta.

EGGPLANT PASTA SAUCE

GF | P | WL

This sauce is spectacular when made with young, tender "baby" aubergines and is a good dish to introduce the vegetable to skeptics. Put it together in the morning and it'll be ready when you come home from work.

Prep Time: 8 h 15 m

Serves: 2

Calories: 835, Sodium: 840 mg, Dietary Fiber: 47.7 g, Total Fat: 5.2 g, Total Carbs: 171.1 g, Protein: 32.4g

INGREDIENTS

....

4 cups courgette, spiralized

4 small ("baby") aubergines or one large one

1 medium yellow onion, chopped

1 28-oz. can Italian-style plum tomatoes

3 large garlic cloves, chopped

1 4-oz can sliced mushrooms, drained

1/3 cup dry red wine

1/3 cup water

1 ½ tsp. Italian seasoning

....

DIRECTIONS

1. Peel eggplant and dice into 1-inch cubes.

2. Spiralize the courgette to make "pasta" (flat rings recommended).

3. Combine all the ingredients except the pasta and olives in a 5 ½ quart slow cooker.

4. Cook on low-heat setting for 8 hours.

5. Boil 4 pints of water in a large saucepan. Blanche the pasta and drain.

6. Stir the olives into the sauce.

7. Divide the hot pasta onto plates and top with sauce.

FETTUCCINE ALFREDO LITE

This luxurious low-carb, low-calorie version of the famously fattening pasta dish will quickly become a favourite.

Prep Time: 15 m

Serves: 2

Calories: 210, Sodium: 232 mg, Dietary Fiber: 2.9 g, Total Fat: 10.4 g, Total Carbs: 14.8 g, Protein: 18.5 g

INGREDIENTS

....

"PASTA"

1 large courgette, spiralized

1 large carrot, spiralized

SAUCE

½ cup plain, non-fat Greek yogurt

½ cup shredded Parmesan cheese

1 Tbsp. olive oil

½ cup water

1 garlic clove minced

1 Tbsp. chopped parsley

¼ tsp black pepper

1/8 tsp ground nutmeg

....

DIRECTIONS

1. Spiralize the courgettes and carrots into thin strands. Heat or cook to your preferences.

2. In a large saucepan, cook the garlic in the olive oil for 1-2 minutes.

3. Add the water to the garlic/oil mixture along with the nutmeg, salt, and pepper. Stir to combine and remove from heat.

4. Add the pasta to the spiced oil mixture, then stir in half the Parmesan cheese.

5. Stir in the yogurt, mixing until everything is creamy.

6. Garnish with the remainder of the Parmesan cheese.

GARLIC SHRIMP & VEGGIE PASTA

Shrimp, though low in calories, are high in cholesterol and should only be eaten as a special treat by those on a weight-loss diet or with high cholesterol. In this dish, the vegetables take center stage while the shrimp chimes in on the doo-wahs.

Prep Time: 20–25 m

Serves: 2

Calories: 418, Sodium: 2,771 mg, Dietary Fiber: 9.2 g, Total Fat: 10.8 g, Total Carbs: 38.5 g, Protein: 39.2 g

INGREDIENTS

....

"PASTA"

4 large broccoli stalks, spiralized

SAUCE

12 oz. small raw shrimp, cleaned and deveined (can use frozen)

1 bell pepper, cut into thin strips

1 bunch asparagus, trimmed and cut into 1-inch pieces

1 cup snow peas (frozen or fresh)

2 garlic cloves, minced

1 tsp. Chinese Five-Spice Powder

1 Tbsp. dark sesame oil

1 Tbsp. soy sauce or tamari

1 ½ cups plain yogurt

1 tsp salt

¼ cup rice vinegar

½ tsp black pepper

....

DIRECTIONS

1. Spiralize the broccoli stalks into thin strands.

2. Boil the veggie "pasta" for 1 minute and then add the shrimp, bell pepper, peas and asparagus.

3. Turn down the heat and simmer for another 4-6 minutes, until the shrimp are cooked. Drain and set aside.

4. Mix the oil, rice vinegar, garlic, Five-Spice powder, and soy sauce.

5. Pour sauce over the pasta and vegetables.

GREEK LAMB PASTA

GF | P | WL

Lamb is an increasingly economical option as chicken prices soar and it pairs well with pasta.

Prep Time: 50–60 m

Serves: 4–6

Calories: 380, Sodium: 267 mg, Dietary Fiber: 6.6 g, Total Fat: 9.2 g, Total Carbs: 45.4 g, Protein: 30.2 g

INGREDIENTS

....

4 cups courgette or yellow squash, spiralized

1 lb. ground lamb

1 4-oz can sliced black olives, drained

1 28-oz. can diced tomatoes

1 small can tomato paste (leave out for Paleo diets)

2 Tbsp. oregano (or Greek seasoning blend)

3 large garlic cloves, minced

1 large yellow onion, diced

1 large bell pepper, diced

Juice of one lemon

3 Tbsp. balsamic vinegar

....

DIRECTIONS

1. In a large saucepan brown the ground lamb. Add the onion, bell pepper, garlic and olives and cook until the onions become translucent.

2. Add the diced tomatoes, lemon juice, vinegar, and spices.

3. Simmer for 10 minutes, then stir in tomato paste.

4. Simmer another 10-20 minutes, adding small amounts of water if the sauce becomes too thick. While simmering, spiralize the courgettes or yellow squashes into flat pasta strands.

5. Ladle over the pasta, wait several minutes to allow the pasta to soften, then serve.

Note: If not following a Paleo diet, sprinkle with a little feta cheese before serving.

GREEK-STYLE PASTA

The combination of salty feta cheese and dry white wine turns this pasta dish into something a little sophisticated. Serve it with slices of roast lamb.

Prep Time: 20 m

Serves: 4

Calories: 173, Sodium: 232 mg, Dietary Fiber: 2.3 g, Total Fat: 11.2 g, Total Carbs: 10.2 g, Protein: 4.2 g

INGREDIENTS

....

"PASTA"

1 large courgette, spiralized

1 large carrot, spiralized

SAUCE

1 large yellow onion, diced

2 garlic cloves, minced

2 Tbsp. olive oil

½ cup dry white wine

½ cup feta cheese,

1 tsp. thyme

1/8 tsp black pepper (to taste)

....

DIRECTIONS

1. Spiralize the courgettes into thin pasta strands. Heat or cook to your preferences.

2. In a large frying pan, brown the onion and garlic in the oil.

3. Pour in the wine and continue to cook over medium heat for 5m minutes.

4. Add the pasta, thyme, and feta cheese t the mixture and stir to combine.

5. Continue cooking until all the flavors have blended and the cheese has melted.

LEMON CHARD PASTA

One of the more colourful "greens," Swiss chard is also one of the world's healthiest foods. In addition to its anti-inflammatory and detoxifying properties, it's known to stabilize blood sugar.

Prep Time: 10–15 m

Serves: 2

Calories: 99, Sodium: 59 mg, Dietary Fiber: 2.8 g, Total Fat: 7.5 g, Total Carbs: 7.9 g, Protein: 2.7 g

INGREDIENTS

....

"PASTA"

1 large courgette, spiralized

SAUCE

1 bunch Swiss chard, chopped roughly

1/8 cup fresh coriander, chopped

2 spring onions, sliced thinly

1 Tbsp. olive oil

1 Tbsp. lemon juice

1 tsp. apple cider vinegar

1 tsp lemon zest

1/4 tsp paprika

1/4 tsp black pepper

....

DIRECTIONS

1. Spiralize the courgette (thin strands recommended). Heat or cook as you prefer.

2. In a large frying pan, sauté the chard in olive oil until limp, around 5 minutes. Remove from pan and set aside in a medium-sized serving bowl.

3. Combine the coriander, vinegar, spring onions, lemon zest, spices, and salt.

4. Combine the pasta and the chard. Add the dressing and "toss" to coat.

PALEO COURGETTE PASTA WITH CHICKEN

Is it possible that when cave men first tasted fowl they thought, "Wow, this tastes like snake?" This is a simple but satisfying dish that can be customized by adding a different palette of spices and herbs.

Prep Time: 15–20 m

Serves: 2–4

Calories: 531, Sodium: 174 mg, Dietary Fiber: 5.0 g, Total Fat: 35.4 g, Total Carbs: 16.3 g, Protein: 43.0 g

INGREDIENTS

....

"PASTA"

8 medium courgettes, spiralized

SAUCE

1 lb. boneless, skinless chicken breast, cut in bite-size pieces

3 Tbsp. coconut oil

1/4 cup sun-dried tomatoes, snipped into strips

1/4 cup virgin olive oil

1/3 cup pine nuts or sliced/slivered almonds

¼ cup lemon juice

1 large garlic clove, minced

1 tsp. arrowroot powder

Zest from ½ lemon

Pepper and salt to taste

....

DIRECTIONS

1. Spiralize the 8 courgettes into thin strands. Heat or cook as you prefer.

2. Melt the coconut oil in a large frying pan, then add the chicken pieces, pepper, garlic, and salt. Brown the chicken pieces, then reduce heat, continuing to sauté them until they're done.

3. Add the pine nuts, sun-dried tomatoes, lemon zest, lemon juice and arrow root powder.

4. Serve chicken and sauce over the "pasta."

Pasta & Cheese with Bacon

This is a grown-up version of Mac n' Cheese, dressed up with two kinds cheese and the salty surprise of bacon. Because bacon makes everything better.

Prep Time: 25 m

Serves: 2

Calories: 1,005, Sodium: 2,253 mg, Dietary Fiber: 5.4 g, Total Fat: 70.8 g, Total Carbs: 25.4 g, Protein: 73.7 g

INGREDIENTS

....

"PASTA"

2 large courgettes, spiralized

2 large carrots, spiralized

SAUCE

6 bacon slices, chopped

¼ cup double cream

2 garlic cloves, minced

Pepper to taste

6 oz. grated Gouda cheese

8 oz. fresh mozzarella, grated

¼ cup fresh basil, chopped (for garnish)

....

DIRECTIONS

1. Spiralize the courgettes and carrots into thin strands. Heat or cook to your preferences.

2. Fry the bacon in a large frying pan over medium heat. When bacon is cooked but not crisp, add the garlic and stir. Continue to cook until the bacon is crisp.

3. Drain off all but a tablespoonful of fat.

4. Add the pasta and the double cream. Reduce heat and stir together until the sauce begins to coat the pasta.

5. Add the cheese and stir until melted.

6. Garnish with chopped basil and fresh-ground pepper.

MAPLE & GARLIC PORK SHOULDER WITH CRISPY SKIN AND SWEET POTATO NOODLES

A rich, crackling, browned skin makes this pork shoulder something truly exceptional. If you add the potato noodles at the end of cooking, they won't get limp and soggy, but will stay crispy and flavorful from the meat drippings.

Servings: 6-8

Prep time: 30 minutes

Cooking time: 18 hours (to roast pork)

Nutritional Info: Calories: 1,111, Sodium: 2,886 mg. Dietary fiber: 4.9 g. Total fat: 59.3 g. Total carbs: 48.9 g. Protein: 89.2 g.

INGREDIENTS

....

2 large potatoes, spiralized

2 large sweet potatoes, spiralized

6-8 pounds bone-in, skin-on pork shoulder

3 Tbsp. fennel seeds

14 garlic cloves, crushed or finely chopped

3 Tbsp. salt

½ cup olive oil

1 tsp. cayenne pepper

1 tsp. black pepper

¾ cup real maple syrup (grade b)

1 large bottle malty, fruity ale

2 tsp. apple cider vinegar

....

DIRECTIONS

1. Allow meat to come up to room temperature, so interior is not cold.

2. Score skin with a very sharp knife, making ½ inch cuts all over surface of skin.

3. Preheat oven to 450.

4. Heat a frying pan on medium heat, and toast fennel seeds, until fragrant, about 3 minutes. Crush seeds in a spice grinder or with a mortar and pestle.

5. Place garlic and salt in a food processor and pulse together to make a paste.

6. Slowly add olive oil, pulse.

7. Add cayenne, black pepper, and ground fennel, and mix well.

8. Rub ⅓ the paste over the skinless side of the meet, then place skin side down on a roasting pan, in the lower half of the oven.

9. Cook for 30 minutes.

10. While cooking, stir the syrup, vinegar, and remaining paste together.

11. Turn the oven down to 225.

12. Flip the shoulder so the skin is up.

13. Rub the remaining paste over the skin side, using a spatula to push into the scores.

14. Return to oven and cook at 225 for 18 hours or longer. If desired, turn heat down to 150 and cook overnight.

15. Pour beer over shoulder several times during cooking, at 3-4 hour intervals.

16. Baste with drippings 2-3 times.

17. 30 minutes before pork is finished cooking, peel potatoes and sweet potatoes and spiralize them into thick strands.

18. Boil a large pot of lightly salted water. Blanche the noodles lightly, approx 3-5 min. Set aside.

19. Immediately prior to serving, add potato noodles to pork pan, mix with drippings, and turn heat back up to 450 and cook for 10 minutes to crisp skin.

20. Put on serving platter, allow to rest 10 minutes, and serve.

PASTA & TURKEY/CHIA MEATBALLS

Even if your only connection to "chia" is that chia pet you had as a kid, trust me; you'll want to add this ingredient to your diet. Chia seeds are practically all fiber and the rest is a healthy mix of Omega-3 fatty acids and other good things.

Prep Time: 50 m

Serves: 2–4

Calories: 355, Sodium: 1139 mg, Dietary Fiber: 8.4 g, Total Fat: 12.5 g, Total Carbs: 20.1 g, Protein: 40.3 g

INGREDIENTS

....

"PASTA"

1 large courgette, spiralized

MEATBALLS

1 lb. lean minced beef or turkey

4 Tbsp. tomato paste

2 Tbsp. chia seeds

3 garlic cloves, minced

2 tsp. oregano

2 tsp. basil

2 tsp olive oil (for sautéing)

1 tsp black pepper

MARINARA

1 medium yellow onion, diced

1 garlic clove, crushed

1 sprig of fresh rosemary, chopped

¼ cup lemon juice

½ cup chicken stock

1 12-oz. can diced tomatoes

1 12-oz, can tomato sauce

½ tsp salt

½ tsp. black pepper

....

DIRECTIONS

1. Make "pasta" out of the courgette (thin strands recommended).

PREPARE CHIA MEATBALLS

1. Mix all the ingredients except the oil. Let sit for 10 minutes.

2. Put the oil in a large frying pan. Shape the meat mixture into small balls (about eight) and brown in the oil, turning each meatball at least 3 times so they brown evenly. Remove the meatballs from heat when they're still slightly rare and set aside.

3. Remove all but 2 Tbsp. fat from the frying pan.

4. Prepare the marinara:

5. Sauté the onion in the frying pan until it's translucent. .

6. Add rosemary and garlic and cook for another 2-4 minutes.

7. Add the lemon juice and chicken stock, then the diced tomatoes, tomato sauce, salt and pepper and mix well.

8. Simmer over medium heat until sauce begins to thicken (about 20 minutes).

9. Reduce heat to low and add meatballs to the pan. Cook 10 minutes, or until meatballs are cooked thoroughly.

10. Divide pasta and sauce between two plates and top with meatballs and sauce.

PASTA ARRABIATA

This extremely simple sauce is deceptively spicy (and you can kick the heat up a notch by just adding more crushed red pepper).

Prep Time: 60 m

Serves: 4

Nutritional Info: Calories: 103, Sodium: 11 mg, Dietary Fiber: 2.8 g, Total Fat: 7.6 g, Total Carbs: 9.3 g, Protein: 2.1 g

INGREDIENTS

....

"PASTA"

4 cups courgette, spiralized

MAIN INGREDIENTS

2 large cans (28-oz) diced tomatoes (don't drain)

4 large garlic cloves, minced

1 bunch fresh basil, chopped (1/3-1/2 cup)

2 tsp. crushed red pepper flakes

2 Tbsp. olive oil

....

DIRECTIONS

1. Combine all the ingredients except the basil and the "pasta" in a large saucepan.

2. Simmer for a half-hour to 45 minutes.

3. Add the basil and simmer for another 10 minutes.

4. While the sauce is on its final simmer, warm the pasta by cooking it for three minutes in a pot of boiling water.

5. Serve immediately, garnished with Parmesan cheese and more pepper flakes if desired.

PASTA PIE

Think of this as the gluten-free equivalent of a quiche. You can make it in minutes, and serve it warm for brunch or at room temperature for a light supper.

Prep Time: 35 m

Serves: 2

Calories: 157, Sodium: 656 mg, Dietary Fiber: 4.3 g, Total Fat: 8.1 g, Total Carbs: 14.5 g, Protein: 10.5 g

INGREDIENTS

....

"PASTA"

3 large courgettes, spiralized

SAUCE

1 ½ cups tomato sauce

½ cup fresh Parmesan cheese, grated

½ cup mozzarella or Monterey Jack cheese, grated

½ cup bell pepper, diced

1 Tbsp. olive oil

5 fresh basil leaves, shredded

....

DIRECTIONS

1. Preheat oven to 325°F.

2. Spiralize the 3 courgettes into thin strands.

3. Mix the "pasta" with the other ingredients and pour into a baking dish that has been treated with cooking spray.

4. Bake for 30 minutes at 325.

5. Remove from oven and let stand on a wire rack for 15 minutes.

6. Serve warm or at room temperature.

PASTA PUTTANESCA

GF | P | WL

This is another classic Italian pasta sauce that is fast and easy to make, yet still full of big flavors.

Prep Time: 30 m

Serves: 2–4

Calories: 413, Sodium: 537 mg, Dietary Fiber: 9.6 g, Total Fat: 8.9 g, Total Carbs: 61.9 g, Protein: 23.5 g

INGREDIENTS

....

4 cups courgette or yellow squash, spiralized

6 anchovies canned in oil (half a 2-oz. can)

1 28-oz. can crushed tomatoes

½ cup pitted black olives, chopped

2 Tbsp. tomato paste

4 garlic cloves, minced

1 tsp. crushed red pepper flakes

1 Tbsp. Italian seasoning

½ small yellow onion, minced

....

DIRECTIONS

1. Spiralize the 4 cups of courgettes or yellow squash into thin strands. Blanche noodles, drain and place in a large bowl.

2. Heat the olive oil in a large saucepan over medium-high heat and sauté the onions until they're soft and translucent, about 4-5 minutes. Add the garlic and the anchovies.

3. Stir and continue to cook. (The anchovies will literally "melt" into the oil.)

4. Add the can of crushed tomatoes (juice and all) along with the tomato paste, Italian seasoning, pepper flakes, and olives.

5. Reduce heat and simmer for 20 minutes.

6. Pour over pasta and toss to coat with sauce.

7. Serve immediately.

Note: Not every Paleo pantry list includes tomato paste, so if you're a hard-core Paleo, you can leave it out. The sauce won't be quite as thick, but will taste fine.

PASTA WITH ANCHOVY SAUCE

GF | P

The anchovies in this sauce dissolve in the oil and leave just their salty, fishy essence behind.

Prep Time: 10–15 m

Serves: 4–6

Calories: 365, Sodium: 1,409 mg, Dietary Fiber: 1.2 g, Total Fat: 36.9 g, Total Carbs: 3.9 g, Protein: 7.1 g

INGREDIENTS

....

4 cups courgette or yellow squash noodles, spiralized

12 anchovy filets, packed in olive oil (2-oz can)

1 cup olive oil

1 Tbsp. crushed red pepper flakes

Juice from one lemon

¼ cup Italian parsley, minced

....

DIRECTIONS

1. Drain oil and mince anchovies.

2. In a small saucepan, heat the minced anchovies in ½ cup olive oil. Stir until the fish "melt" into the oil (about 5 minutes).

3. Stir in the pepper flakes and the rest of the olive oil.

4. Add the lemon juice and stir.

5. Pour the hot sauce over the raw noodles and mix together.

PASTA CAJUN STYLE

There are lots of different "Cajun spice" mixtures on the market, some spicier than others. Start off with half the amount of seasoning if you have a low tolerance for heat; you can always add more if necessary.

Prep Time: 25–30 m

Serves: 2–4

Calories: 405, Sodium: 1,299 mg, Dietary Fiber: 5.1 g, Total Fat: 23.8 g, Total Carbs: 21.2 g, Protein: 27.5 g

INGREDIENTS

....

"PASTA"

4 large courgettes, spiralized

CAJUN SAUCE

½ cup canned coconut milk

2 Andouille-style sausages cooked and cut into ½ inch pieces

8 oz. raw shrimp, deveined

½ red bell pepper, chopped

½ green bell pepper, chopped

3 Tbsp. olive oil

2 garlic cloves, crushed

½ yellow onion, diced

3 Tbsp. Cajun Spice Mix

....

DIRECTIONS

1. Spiralize the courgettes into thin strands of pasta. Heat or cook as you prefer.

2. In a large frying pan, heat the olive oil over medium heat.

3. Sauté the onions and peppers with 1 tablespoon of Cajun spice mix. When the vegetables are tender and the onions, translucent, set aside in a bowl.

4. Add the shrimp and another tablespoon of the spice mix to the same pan and sauté until the shrimp are cooked through. Add the cooked shrimp to the sautéed vegetables in the bowl.

5. Add the sausage pieces to the frying pan, along with the last tablespoon of Cajun spice. Sauté until the sausage is cooked thoroughly. Add the sausage to the bowl of ingredients on the side.

6. Heat the coconut milk in a large saucepan, stirring until it begins to thicken slightly. Add the other cooked ingredients and mix well.

7. Serve sauce over the pasta.

Note: If Andouille sausage is not available in your area you can substitute any spicy, sausage, including hot Italian-style chicken sausage.

PASTA WITH EGGPLANT & CHARRED TOMATO SAUCE

This easy pasta takes a lot less time to prepare than its carb-heavy cousin Moussaka. It can be lightened up even more by using part-skim ricotta.

Prep Time: 75 m

Serves: 2

Calories: 199, Sodium: 53 mg, Dietary Fiber: 5.7 g, Total Fat: 13.0 g, Total Carbs: 18.1 g, Protein: 6.8 g

INGREDIENTS

....

"PASTA"

1 large courgette, spiralized

SAUCE

¼ large eggplant, diced

2 Tomatoes, seeded and diced

4 large garlic cloves, peeled

1 ½ Tbsp. olive oil

¼ yellow onion, diced

5 basil leaves, chopped

3 Tbsp. ricotta cheese

....

DIRECTIONS

1. Preheat oven to 325° F.

2. Spiralize courgette into thin strands.

3. Wrap 5 peeled garlic cloves in aluminum foil, along with a pinch of salt and a ½ teaspoon of olive oil. Bake garlic for 40-50 minutes, until browned and soft.

4. Sauté the diced eggplant until soft (10-12 minutes) in a large frying pan using the other 1 Tbsp. olive oil. Set cooked eggplant aside.

5. Using the same pan, combine 2 of the roasted garlic cloves, the diced tomatoes, and the diced onion. Cook for 2-4 minutes, adding more olive oil if necessary.

6. Remove from heat and blend into a smooth paste in a food processor.

7. Combine the tomato mixture, the remaining garlic, and the pasta and cook over medium heat for another 2-4 minutes.

8. Garnish with the ricotta cheese and chopped basil.

PASTA WITH LEMON & RICOTTA

GF | WL | V

In Italy, pasta is often served in small portions as a separate course; feel free to repurpose this creamy pasta dish as a side.

Prep Time: 20 m

Serves: 2

Calories: 672, Sodium: 263 mg, Dietary Fiber: 5.1 g, Total Fat: 22.6 g, Total Carbs: 91.6 g, Protein: 30.1 g

INGREDIENTS

....

4 cups courgette or yellow squash, spiralized

4 pints water

1 8-oz. container ricotta cheese

¼ oz butter, cut into pieces

½ cup chopped flat-leaf parsley

½ tsp. black pepper

Zest from one lemon

....

DIRECTIONS

1. Bring the water to boil in a large saucepan while spiralizing the courgette or yellow squash into thin strands.

2. Boil the pasta for 1-2 minutes until tender. Remove 1 cup of water from the pasta pot.

3. Combine the cheese, butter and reserved pasta water, whisking until creamy.

4. Drain the pasta and put in a large serving bowl.

5. Add the parsley, pepper, lemon zest and the cream toss.

6. Toss with tongs to mix.

7. Serve immediately.

PASTA WITH RICOTTA & BACON

GF

You can prepare this pasta and sauce in less time than it takes to have a pizza delivered, and it's a lot better for you!

Prep Time: 55–60 m

Serves: 4

Calories: 353, Sodium: 269 mg, Dietary Fiber: 5.7 g, Total Fat: 7.9 g, Total Carbs: 55.3 g, Protein: 17.4 g

INGREDIENTS

....

4 cups courgette, spiralized

2 slices bacon, chopped

1 medium yellow onion, diced

1 medium bell pepper, diced

2 large garlic cloves, crushed

1 28-oz. can diced tomatoes

½ cup ricotta cheese

....

DIRECTIONS

1. Spiralize the courgettes into flat rings.
2. Blanche noodles, drain and place in a large bowl.

3. Heat a heavy stockpot over medium heat and fry the bacon until it is beginning to crisp.

4. Add the onions and peppers and cook until the onions are translucent, then add the garlic and cook for another minute.

5. Add the can of tomatoes, juice and all.

6. Simmer for 20 minutes (or longer) to blend flavors.

7. Add the cheese to the tomato sauce and stir.

8. Add the cooked pasta to the saucepot and stir to blend.

9. Serve immediately.

Note: If you have some spinach on hand, add about a cup of spinach leaves to give the sauce a little extra fiber.

PESTO PASTA & SAUSAGES

The pesto here is made without Parmesan (a Paleo no-no) but with the addition of almonds for a second helping of nutty nutrition.

Prep Time: 20 m

Serves: 2–4

Calories: 453, Sodium: 657 mg, Dietary Fiber: 3.7 g, Total Fat: 35.5 g, Total Carbs: 11.4 g, Protein: 25.7 g

INGREDIENTS

....

"PASTA"

3 medium courgettes, spiralized

SAUCE

1 cup fresh basil leaves

1/4 cup Walnuts

1/4 cup Almonds

4 spicy Italian chicken sausages, cut into bite-size pieces

5 to 6 garlic cloves

1 medium red bell pepper, diced

3 Tbsp. olive oil

....

DIRECTIONS

1. Spiralize the courgettes into thin strands. Heat or cook as you prefer.

2. Toast nuts for 3-4 minutes, then set aside to cool.

3. Combine the nuts, basil, olive oil, garlic and salt and process in a blender until smooth.

4. Cut sausages into small pieces and sauté them in a medium saucepan.

5. Add the "pasta" and bell peppers to the sausages. Stir in the pesto sauce. Serve hot.

PESTO COURGETTE PASTA WITH SAUSAGE

Pesto sauce is traditionally made with pine nuts, but this recipe uses walnuts.

Prep Time: 15 m

Serves: 2–3

Nutritional Info: Calories: 390, Sodium: 313 mg, Dietary Fiber: 4.6 g, Total Fat: 34.2 g, Total Carbs: 12.6 g, Protein: 14.3 g

INGREDIENTS

....

"PASTA"

3 Courgette, spiralized

SAUCE

1 pkg. hot Italian chicken sausage

1 cup fresh basil

½-3/4 cup walnut pieces

4 large garlic cloves, minced

1 green bell pepper, seeded and diced

4 Tbsp. olive oil

Dash salt

....

DIRECTIONS

1. Chop the sausages into bite-size pieces and brown in a non-stick pan. Set aside.

2. Combine all the other in the bowl of a food processor and blend until smooth.

3. Spiralize the courgette (flat strands recommended).

4. Warm the courgette pasta in boiling water, drain, and put in a large bowl.

5. Toss with the pesto sauce and cooked pieces of sausage.

6. Serve immediately.

Note: Chunks of skinless chicken breast can be substituted for the sausage. Add the onions and peppers and cook until the onions are translucent, then add the garlic and cook for another minute.

PIZZA PASTA

This combination of pizza fixins' and veggie "pasta" lightens the glycemic load of everybody's favorite "junk food" fix. If calories aren't a consideration, top with some shredded mozzarella and microwave for 30 seconds to get the full-on pizza "experience."

Prep Time: 35–40 m

Serves: 2

Calories: 446, Sodium: 1,494 mg, Dietary Fiber: 13.1 g, Total Fat: 14.3 g, Total Carbs: 55.2 g, Protein: 27.4 g

INGREDIENTS

....

"PASTA"

2 large courgettes or 2 large carrots, spiralized

PIZZA SAUCE

2 Italian chicken chicken sausages

14-oz. jar pizza sauce

1 cup large yellow onion, diced

1 cup sliced mushrooms

1 bell pepper, diced

1/4 cup sliced black olives

4 garlic cloves, minced

1 tsp. olive oil

....

DIRECTIONS

1. Spiralize the courgettes or carrots into thin strands. Heat or cook as you prefer.

2. Cut the sausages into 1-inch pieces and sauté in a medium frying pan. Set aside.

3. Add the olive oil to a large saucepan.

4. Cook the onions until they are translucent, then add the diced pepper and sliced mushrooms. Cook for another 5 minutes.

5. Mix in the cooked sausage pieces.

6. Add the pizza sauce and stir over medium heat for another 5 minutes.

7. Pour over the "pasta" and garnish with sliced olives.

PUMPKIN PASTA WITH BACON & GREENS

This is a variation of one of the simplest and most decadent pasta dishes ever invented. The pumpkin pairs exceptionally well with the smoky bacon, but you can use any veggie pasta you like.

Prep Time: 20 m

Serves: 4–8

Nutritional Info: Calories: 321, Sodium: 1344 mg, Dietary Fiber: 1.1 g, Total Fat: 24.0 g, Total Carbs: 3.2 g, Protein: 22.4 g

INGREDIENTS

....

"PASTA"

4 cups pumpkin, warmed & spiralized

SAUCE

1lb o r 454 gms bacon

4 large garlic cloves, chopped

1 bunch spinach, shredded

1 Tbsp. dried red pepper flakes (or to taste)

....

DIRECTIONS

1. Fry the bacon until crisp. Remove from heat and put aside to cool.

2. Sauté the chopped garlic in the remaining bacon fat until it is golden brown.

3. Add the dried pepper flakes.

4. Spiralize the pumpkin into flat strands. Warm them (sauté, blanche, microwave, or boil).

5. Combine the warmed pasta and the shredded spinach.

6. Pour the bacon mixture over the pasta and spinach and mix well.

7. Serve immediately.

Note: The combination of hot bacon fat and spinach will remind diners of classic "wilted salads," while the nuttiness of the garlic and the heat of the pepper will cut the richness of the bacon fat.

QUICK SPAGHETTI WITH MEAT SAUCE

Lean protein and non-starchy vegetables are an unbeatable combination when you're trying to lose weight. This simple, classic "spaghetti" with meat sauce is so flavorful you won't even notice you're getting a double-dose of vegetables on your plate.

Prep Time: 25–35 m

Serves: 2

Calories: 466, Sodium: 1,092 mg, Dietary Fiber: 11.3 g, Total Fat: 17.4 g, Total Carbs: 35.2 g, Protein: 44.3 g

INGREDIENTS

....

"PASTA"

2 large courgettes, spiralized

1 large carrot, spiralized

SAUCE

½ lb. lean turkey or beef

1 12-oz. can crushed tomatoes

1 medium yellow onion, diced

1 Small celery stalk, diced

2 garlic cloves, crushed

1 Tbsp. Italian seasoning

212

1 Tbsp. olive oil

½ tsp salt

Parmesan cheese for topping

....

DIRECTIONS

1. Spiralize the courgettes and carrot into thin pasta strands. Heat or cook to your preferences.

2. In a large saucepan, sauté the onion and celery until the onion begins to get brown (5-9 minutes).

3. Stir in the Italian seasoning and the garlic and cook for another minute.

4. Push the vegetables to the side and add the minced beef. Cook until the meat is well done.

5. Add the tomatoes and simmer until sauce is thickened. Adjust seasoning and serve over warmed "pasta."

6. Garnish with Parmesan cheese.

PASTA WITH CLAMS

This is a tasty and quick variation of a classic Italian specialty. If you like the sauce extra spicy, add 1 Tbsp. of crushed red pepper to the sauce as it's getting its final simmer.

Prep Time: 45–50 m

Serves: 2

Calories: 309, Sodium: 1,361 mg, Dietary Fiber: 7.5 g, Total Fat: 15.1 g, Total Carbs: 37.3 g, Protein: 7.3 g

INGREDIENTS

....

"PASTA"

2 large courgettes or 1 large carrot, spiralized

SAUCE

½ lb. littleneck clams

1 12-oz. jar spicy tomato sauce

2 Tbsp. olive oil

¼ cup dry white wine

1 garlic clove, minced

1 Tbsp. chopped basil

....

DIRECTIONS

1. Spiralize the courgettes or carrot into thin strands. Heat or cook as you prefer.

2. Inspect clams and discard any with chipped or wide-open shells. If shells are partially open, tap on the shells to see if they close. If they do not, discard the clams.

3. Place clams in a large bowl and cover with cold water. Let soak for 25 minutes. Pull the clams one by one from the now-dirty water, and rinse individually while scrubbing the shells to remove any remaining debris or sand. Repeat until all the clams are cleaned.

4. Refrigerate clams.

5. Add the olive oil to a large saucepan and cook the garlic and onions until they are soft but not brown, about 1 minute.

6. Add the white wine and bring to a boil.

7. Add the cleaned clams (in their shells), cover and cook for 5-8 minutes until the shells have opened. Don't overcook; if a shell hasn't opened after 8 minutes, it's not going to, so discard it.

8. Remove the clams and set aside.

9. Strain the wine/clam broth and combine it with the tomato sauce in a medium saucepan. Bring to a boil.

10. Reduce heat, add the basil, and simmer for another 5 minutes.

11. Combine the sauce and the clams and serve over the "pasta."

PORCINI AND ROSEMARY CRUSTED BEEF SIRLOIN WITH PORT WINE SAUCE AND POTATO LINGUINI

The rich umami flavor of the mushrooms, combined with the slightly acidic sweetness of the port wine sauce makes this dish something exceptional. Frying the potato linguini gives it a bit of crunch to compliment the meat.

Servings: 6-8

Prep time: 20 minutes

Cooking time: 1 hour

Nutritional Info: Calories: 647, Sodium: 255 mg. Dietary fiber: 7.3 g. Total fat: 21.9 g. Total carbs: 43.7 g. Protein: 55.0 g.

INGREDIENTS

....

POTATO LINGUINI

5-6 large russet potatoes, spiralized

1 Tbsp. butter

Salt to taste

TENDERLOIN

3 pounds beef sirloin

1 oz dried porcini mushrooms

2 Tbsp. fresh rosemary leaves, chopped finely

1 tsp. black peppercorns

Olive oil

Salt to taste

SAUCE

½ oz dried porcini mushrooms

¾ cup water

3 Tbsp. unsalted butter, divided

1 medium shallot, chopped finely

1 cup port wine

1 cup heavy bodied red wine

2 rosemary springs

Salt to taste

....

DIRECTIONS

TENDERLOIN

1. Salt tenderloin well, all over.

2. Refrigerate, covered, for at least 4 hours, but not more than 24 hours.

3. 30 minutes before roasting, remove from refrigerator to allow to come up to room temperature.

4. Preheat oven to 400.

5. Combine mushrooms, rosemary, and peppercorns in a spice grinder or food processor (make sure mushrooms are totally dry so they pulverize well.)

6. Grind to a coarse powder.

7. Rub beef with olive oil, then rub with mushroom rosemary powder.

8. Heat 1 tablespoon oil in a heavy bottomed frying pan.

9. Sear all sides of beef till brown and slightly crispy.

10. Transfer to a roasting pan. Roast until meat thermometer in the thickest part reads 125 degrees (about 30 minutes).

11. Remove from oven and transfer to a cutting board.

12. Tent with foil and let rest for 15 minutes.

POTATO LINGUINI

1. Spiralize potatoes, skin on, thick strand cut.

2. Boil a large pot of lightly salted water, and add potatoes.

3. Boil till tender, but not falling apart, 5-8 minutes.

4. Drain very well.

5. Reheat pan used to brown the meat, and make the sauce base over medium heat.

6. Add 1 tablespoon butter, and melt.

7. Add potatoes to pan, and sauté lightly, till slightly crispy. Set aside while making sauce.

SAUCE

1. Reconstitute the mushrooms: place mushrooms in water for about 20 minutes, till swelled.

2. Strain liquid through a paper towel or coffee filter into a small bowl, reserving liquid.

3. Coarsely chop mushrooms.

4. In the frying pan used for browning the meat, add 1 tablespoon butter, shallots, and chopped mushrooms.

5. Sauté over medium heat until shallots are soft and translucent 2-5 minutes.

6. Add port wine to deglaze the pan, scraping up all browned bits.

7. Add red wine, mushroom liquid, and rosemary.

8. Bring to a boil and cook on high, uncovered, until sauce has reduced by about half to roughly 1 ½ cups.

9. Add salt to taste.

10. Strain through a fine-meshed sieve, pushing on all solids to drain liquid.

11. Discard solids and put sauce back in a small sauce pan over medium heat.

12. Whisk in 2 tablespoons butter, slowly.

13. Set aside, on warm.

ASSEMBLING THE DISH

1. Cut rested tenderloin, diagonal to the grain, in ¼ inch slices.

2. Make a nest of potato linguini on the plate, top with sliced tenderloin.

3. Dress with port wine sauce.

4. Serve warm.

ROSEMARY & TOMATO PASTA

Rosemary is the go-to herb in Greek cooking, but it's also a major ingredient in the blend known as Herbes de Provence. A little of the aromatic plant goes a long way, so don't get carried away. You want just enough to "perfume" your dish, not overwhelm it.

Prep Time: 20 m

Serves: 2–4

Calories: 283, Sodium: 477 mg, Dietary Fiber: 6.5 g, Total Fat: 18.8 g, Total Carbs: 23.8 g, Protein: 9.6 g

INGREDIENTS

....

"PASTA"

4 large courgettes, spiralized

2 large carrots, spiralized

SAUCE

½ yellow onion, diced

1 tsp. dried rosemary

4 garlic cloves, crushed

¼ cup olive oil

1 14.5-oz. large can of stewed, delete comma whole tomatoes, drained and finely chopped

....

DIRECTIONS

1. Spiralize the courgettes into thin pasta strands. Heat or cook to your preferences.

2. Combine the rest of the ingredients in a blender or food processor and combine until smooth.

3. Pour the tomato mixture into a medium saucepan and heat over medium, stirring frequently, for 10 minutes.

4. Top pasta with the sauce and serve.

SMOKED SALMON PASTA WITH LEMON & DILL

GF

This delicious pasta works as the centerpiece for a Sunday brunch or as a light supper with a side salad and a nice glass of the white wine used in the sauce.

Prep Time: 25 m

Serves: 2

Calories: 902, Sodium: 1282 mg, Dietary Fiber: 12.6 g, Total Fat: 32.1 g, Total Carbs: 111.1 g, Protein: 36.0 g

INGREDIENTS

....

4 cups courgette or yellow squash, spiralized

1 4-oz. package smoked salmon, cut in strips

½ cup dry white wine

¼ cup fresh dill, chopped

1 small red onion, minced

3 Tbsp. olive oil

½ cup and half

1 8-oz package frozen peas, thawed and drained

1 lemon cut in wedges

....

DIRECTIONS

1. Spiralize courgette or yellow squash into flat strands.

2. Blanche noodles, drain and place in a large bowl.

3. In a large frying pan, heat the oil and sauté the onion until it is soft and translucent.

4. Add the white wine to the frying pan, reduce heat, and simmer until it is reduced in volume and beginning to thicken.

5. Add the peas and then the half and half, stirring gently.

6. Simmer for 3 more minutes, then add the salmon and dill.

7. Heat through and stir until the sauce has thickened a little more.

8. Pour the sauce over the pasta in the serving bowl and toss to blend.

9. Serve immediately, garnished with lemon wedges.

Note: This dish can be made with canned or leftover poached salmon if you prefer.

SPAGHETTI WITH OLIVE OIL, SPINACH & PUMPKIN SEEDS

Pumpkin seeds, also known as "pepitas," have a surprisingly assertive flavor despite their small size. They are a good source of zinc, which boosts the immune system and also regulates testosterone levels.

Prep Time: 15 m

Serves: 2

Calories: 437, Sodium: 194 mg, Dietary Fiber: 7.1 g, Total Fat: 36.5 g, Total Carbs: 24.8 g, Protein: 11.5 g

INGREDIENTS

....

"PASTA"

2 large courgettes, spiralized

2 large carrots, spiralized

SAUCE

2 ½ cups spinach leaves, shredded

1/3 cup pumpkin seeds

3 garlic cloves, crushed

¼ cup olive oil

Pinch of salt

....

DIRECTIONS

1. Spiralize the courgettes and carrots into thin strands.

2. Combine the spinach, pumpkin seeds, garlic, olive oil and salt in a blender and process until smooth.

3. Serve over the pasta.

ROASTED BABY TURNIPS WITH DIJON-SHALLOT VINAIGRETTE AND BEET NOODLES

This very simple side dish is filled with color and flavor. For added attractiveness, use half golden beetroot, half red beetroot. Best served at room temperature, this dish is easy enough to make in a pinch, but tastes as though you worked all day.

Servings: 4-6

Prep time: 10 minutes

Cooking time: 30 minutes

Nutritional Info: Calories: 137, Sodium: 82 mg. Dietary fiber: 1.1 g. Total fat: 13.3 g. Total carbs: 5.1 g. Protein: 0.7 g.

INGREDIENTS

....

1 bunch baby red beetroot, peeled & spiralized

2 bunches baby turnips, peeled and chopped into quarters

2 Tbsp. olive oil

Salt and pepper to taste

DRESSING

2 Tbsp. white wine vinegar

1 Tbsp. Dijon mustard

¼ cup extra virgin olive oil

1 shallot, finely minced

1 Tbsp. chopped tarragon

Salt and pepper to taste

....

DIRECTIONS

TURNIPS

1. Preheat oven to 400 degrees.

2. Toss turnips in olive oil and salt and pepper.

3. Spread in a single layer on a baking sheet and bake 10-15 minutes, or until softened inside, slightly brown and caramelized outside.

BEETROOT

1. Spiralize beetroot into thin strands.

2. Boil a pot of lightly salted water.

3. Add spiral cut beetroot and blanche until just soft 5-7 minutes.

4. Drain and set aside.

DRESSING

1. Either using a blender or a hand whisk, whisk together vinegar and mustard.

2. Slowly add the olive oil, in a thin stream, and whisk till emulsified.

3. Whisk in minced shallots.

ASSEMBLING THE DISH

1. Toss the turnips with the dressing.

2. Plate on a bed of beet noodles.

3. Serve at room temperature.

SPICY SHRIMP WITH VEGETABLE NOODLES AND BABY SPINACH

The heat of this dish can be easily adjusted by adding or subtracting the amount of sriracha. Tabletop grills make an excellent substitute for a traditional barbecue if one is unavailable. Either way, grilling vastly improves the shrimp's taste, and serving over vegetable noodles gives a unique, light, fresh flavor.

Servings: 2-3

Prep time: at least 2 hours (for marinade)

Cooking time: 15 minutes

Nutritional Info: Calories: 534, Sodium: 695 mg. Dietary fiber: 5.0 g. Total fat: 23.2 g. Total carbs: 24.8 g. Protein: 62.8 g.

INGREDIENTS

....

1 large courgette, spiralized

1 large yellow squash, spiralized

2 pounds large shrimp, peeled and deveined

1 bunch baby spinach, rinsed well

⅓ cup sriracha

⅓ cup olive oil

1 tsp. Worcestershire sauce

3 garlic cloves, crushed

231

1 bunch coriander, roughly chopped, plus more for garnish

1 tsp. sugar

Salt and pepper to taste

....

DIRECTIONS

MARINADE

1. In a mixing bowl, combine sriracha, olive oil, Worcestershire sauce, garlic, coriander, and sugar. Add salt and pepper to taste.

2. Reserve ¼ cup marinade.

3. Put in a 1 gallon plastic bag, and add shrimp, mix well.

4. Marinate in the refrigerator for at least 2 hours, longer marinating time will improve flavor.

VEGETABLE NOODLES

1. Spiralize courgette and squash into thin strands.

2. Heat a large pot of lightly salted water to boiling.

3. Toss in noodles and spinach together, and blanche for 2-3 minutes until just softened.

4. Drain well, and sprinkle a few drops of virgin olive oil over top.

ASSEMBLING THE DISH

1. Heat the barbecue. (If no barbecue available, a tabletop grill can be used).

2. Remove the shrimp from the marinade, and skewer, filling the skewers within ½ inch of each end.

3. Grill each skewer until pink, approximately 3-5 minutes a side.

4. Toss vegetable mixture with reserved marinade, until lightly coated.

5. Serve shrimp skewers on a bed of vegetable noodles and spinach.

ROSEMARY PORK RAGOUT WITH SWEET POTATO PASTA

This pork ragout is delicious served with any type of pasta. However, the spiralized sweet potato pasta takes it up another notch, combining deep rosemary and pork flavors with the starchy sweetness of sweet potato. Guaranteed to transform a cold evening into a delight one.

Servings: 4

Prep Time: 3.5 h

Nutritional Info: Calories: 708, Sodium: 431 mg, Dietary Fiber: 18.3 g, Total Fat: 12.9 g, Total Carbs: 99.3 g, Protein: 48.4 g

INGREDIENTS

....

"PASTA"

4-6 sweet potatoes, peeled & spiralized

SAUCE

1 large yellow onion, roughly chopped

1 2-pound pork roast

3 sprigs fresh rosemary, chopped (or 3 tsp. dried rosemary)

2 large garlic cloves, minced

1 large (35-oz) can crushed tomatoes (no salt)

Dash freshly ground black pepper

3 Tbsp. olive oil

....

DIRECTIONS

1. Heat the olive oil in a heavy frying pan and sear the pork roast on all sides.

2. Remove the meat from the pan and set aside.

3. Combine the garlic, onion and chopped rosemary and sauté in the remaining olive oil until the onion is translucent.

4. Combine the rosemary mixture with the meat in a large saucepan.

5. Pour in the crushed tomatoes, juice and all.

6. Add the seared pork loin.

7. Bring the liquid to a boil, then cover and reduce heat.

8. Simmer until the pork begins to fall apart (about 3 hours).

9. Remove the cooked meat from the liquid and let cool slightly.

10. Shred the meat and return to the pot, simmering another five minutes until everything has warmed up again.

11. Add the dried pepper flakes.

12. Spiralize the pumpkin into nice pasta ribbons. Warm them (sauté, blanche, microwave, or boil).

13. Combine the warmed pasta and the shredded spinach.

PASTA

1. Spiralize the sweet potatoes into thick strands. Prepare or cook according to your preference. (Don't overcook or they'll get mushy).

2. Pour the Ragout over the pasta and garnish with additional rosemary sprigs if desired.

3. Serve immediately.

Note: The leftover ragout makes an excellent variation on the "Sloppy Joe" sandwich filling. A good gluten-free bun option is Udi's Gluten-Free hamburger buns.

SEARED SCALLOPS WITH SPRING ONION, TARRAGON CREAM AND VEGETABLE NOODLES

Delicious as either an appetizer or a main course, the buttery taste of the scallops is cut very well with the anise-flavor of the tarragon in the cream sauce. The almond flour allows this recipe to remain gluten free while still thickening properly. If almond flour isn't easily available, a little bit of rice flour can be substituted.

Servings: 4 as main course, 6 as appetizer

Prep time: 15 minutes

Cooking time: 45 minutes

Nutritional Info: Calories: 146, Sodium: 84 mg. Dietary fiber: 1.4 g. Total fat: 12.9 g. Total carbs: 6.3 g. Protein: 3.2 g.

INGREDIENTS

....

1 large courgette, spiralized

1 large yellow squash, spiralized

1lb o r 454 gms wild sea scallops

4 Tbsp. unsalted butter

1 Tbsp. almond or rice flour

1 cup whole milk

1 bunch spring onions

2 Tbsp. fresh tarragon leaves

Grapeseed or olive oil

2 Tbsp. creme fraiche

Fresh chives for garnish

Salt and pepper to taste

....

DIRECTIONS

SAUCE

1. Chop spring onions — coarsely chop greens, finely dice the bulbs

2. Melt the butter in a heavy bottomed sauce pan over medium heat

3. Add the diced onion bulbs, and ½ Tbsp. salt

4. Reduce heat to low, and cook 20-25 minutes until very soft and tender

5. Add the chopped green tops, mix well, and cook 5-10 more minutes until the tops have softened but retain the bright green color.

6. Sprinkle the flour over the onions and butter, and cook for 2-3 minutes, until the flour no longer smells raw

7. Raise heat to medium, and add the milk.

8. Cook for several minutes, until just thickened

9. Add the tarragon and stir well.

10. Turn off the heat and either pour mixture into a blender, or use an immersion blender to blend until very smooth.

11. Return to pan, turn heat on low, and cook several more minutes until mixture is thick enough to coat a spoon.

12. Take off the heat, and whisk in creme fraiche.

SCALLOPS

1. Place the scallops on a plate, and refrigerate uncovered for about 30 minutes. (Prepare spiralized vegetables during this time).

2. Lightly grease a heavy-bottomed frying pan with grapeseed or olive oil and heat over medium high heat until shiny, but not popping.

3. Pat the scallops dry, then place them in the pan, being careful not to crowd them.

4. Sear them 2-4 minutes on a side until they are brown and slightly crispy and caramelized. They are done when they come off the pan easily, but should be soft in the middle.

5. Set aside.

NOODLES

1. While scallops are being refrigerated, spiralize the courgette and squash into thin rings.

2. Boil a pot of lightly salted water.

3. Add the vegetables, and blanche until just tender, approximately 2-3 minutes.

4. Drain well and set aside.

ASSEMBLING THE DISH

1. In shallow bowls or soup plates, create a nest of vegetable noodles.

2. Spoon sauce, several tablespoons per plate.

3. Place scallops on top.

4. Serve hot.

TURKEY PIE WITH SPAGHETTI CRUST

GF

The veggie spaghetti crust can be adapted to work with any quiche. It is cheese-heavy, though, so it's not suitable for Paleo or Weight-loss diets.

Prep Time: 55 m

Serves: 4

Calories: 408, Sodium: 561 mg, Dietary Fiber: 2.4 g, Total Fat: 18.9 g, Total Carbs: 29.8 g, Protein: 32.3 g

INGREDIENTS

....

2 cups courgette, spiralized

¼ pound ground turkey

¼ oz butter

1 egg, beaten

¼ cup fresh grated Parmesan cheese

1 cup cottage cheese

2 tbsp. butter, divided

1 egg, beaten

2 tbsp. grated Parmesan cheese

2/3 c. low fat cottage cheese

1/2 c. each diced onion & green pepper

5 oz. cooked ground turkey, crumbled

241

1 c. canned Italian tomatoes (with liquid), drained & chopped, reserving liquid

1/4 c. tomato sauce

1 tsp. each sugar & oregano

1/2 tsp. salt

Dash each garlic powder & pepper

4 oz. Mozzarella cheese, shredded

....

DIRECTIONS

1. Preheat oven to 350 degrees.

2. Coat 9" pie pan with butter or non-stick cooking spray and set aside. Melt 1 tablespoon butter.

3. In 1 quart bowl combine spaghetti, egg, Parmesan cheese and melted butter, mixing well.

4. Press spaghetti mixture over bottom and up sides of sprayed pan to form a crust. Spread cottage cheese over crust.

5. In frying pan heat remaining butter, add onion and green pepper and sauté until soft.

6. Add remaining ingredients except Mozzarella cheese and stir to combine.

7. Reduce heat and simmer about ten minutes.

8. Spread mixture evenly over cottage cheese and bake 15 to 20 minutes. Sprinkle pie with Mozzarella and bake until lightly brown, about 5 minutes longer.

9. Remove from oven and let stand 5 minutes before slicing.

SPICY VEGETABLE NOODLES WITH KALE AND PEANUT SAUCE

A tasty dish with just a bit of heat, this recipe is easily scaled to any number of servings. Double (or triple!) it to have a main or side dish for any event. It can also be made vegetarian by simply removing the fish sauce, and replacing it with a dash of salt.

Servings: 1

Prep time: 20 minutes

Cooking time: 10 minutes

Nutritional Info: Calories: 331, Sodium: 1,848 mg. Dietary fiber: 7.3 g. Total fat: 19.3 g. Total carbs: 29.6 g. Protein: 16.9 g.

INGREDIENTS

....

1 medium courgette, spiralized

1 medium yellow squash, spiralized

1/2 tsp. sesame oil

2 tsp. gluten free soy sauce

1 tsp. sriracha

1/8 tsp. fish sauce, plus more to taste

2 Tbsp. peanut butter

1/2 bunch kale, de-ribbed and sliced into bite-sized pieces

Chopped scallions, for garnish

Chili flakes, for garnish

Chopped peanuts, for garnish

....

DIRECTIONS

NOODLES

1. Spiralize courgette and squash into thick strands.

2. Heat a large pot of lightly salted water to boiling.

3. Add vegetables and boil till just soft, about 2-3 minutes.

4. Remove from heat, and drain, reserving 3 tablespoons of water.

SAUCE

1. In a frying pan, over medium-low heat, mix sesame oil, soy sauce, sriracha, and fish sauce.

2. Stir to combine, and let cook for about 30 seconds.

3. Add peanut butter, stir well.

4. Add 1-3 tablespoons of reserved water, until sauce is desired thickness, then turn off heat.

ASSEMBLING THE DISH

1. Heat a large pot of water to boiling.

2. Add kale, and blanche for 15-30 seconds, until just softened.

3. Drain well, and add to pan containing sauce.

4. Place vegetable noodles in a serving dish and cover with warm sauce with kale.

5. Garnish with chopped scallions, peanuts, and chili flakes.

VEGETABLE PASTA WITH CHICKEN PICCATA

The Cuisique vegetable cutter is the best friend a gluten-free gourmet can have. Vegetable "pasta" is far more satisfying than other substitutes for wheat noodles, and much more nutritious.

Prep Time: 35 m

Serves: 4

Calories: 604, Sodium: 483 mg, Dietary Fiber: 9.3 g, Total Fat: 25.0 g, Total Carbs: 42.6 g, Protein: 53.7 g

INGREDIENTS

....

"PASTA"

3 large courgettes, spiralized

3 large carrots, spiralized

SAUCE

4 boneless, skinless chicken breast halves

1 cup cherry tomatoes, halved

1 large red bell pepper, cut in ¼-inch strips

1½ cups fat-free, low-sodium stock

1 ¼ cups yellow squash, cut in matchsticks

2 garlic cloves, minced

¾ cup grated Parmesan cheese

1 small yellow onion, thinly sliced

½ cup fresh basil, shredded

2 Tbsp olive oil

½ cup gluten-free flour

1 Tbsp butter

6 Tbsp. lemon juice

½ cup spring onions, sliced thin

....

DIRECTIONS

1. Spiralize the courgettes and carrots into thin strands.

2. Bring a quart of water to a boil in a medium saucepan and boil the Veggetti for 3 minutes. Drain but reserve a cup of the cooking water.

3. In a large frying pan, sauté onion and bell pepper for 7-9 minutes or until they start to brown. Transfer vegetables to a medium-sized bowl and keep warm.

4. Add the squash to the pan and sauté until tender/crisp, about 4 minutes.

5. Add the garlic and tomatoes to the squash, and continue to sauté for another 2 minutes.

6. Mix in the cooked onions and pepper.

7. Add the pasta and reserved "pasta" water to the vegetable mix. Stir in the basil and ½ cup of Parmesan.

8. Meanwhile, combine the gluten-free flour with the salt and pepper in a large Ziplock bag. Add the chicken breasts and shake to coat with the flour mixture.

9. Brown the chicken in 1 tablespoon olive oil.

10. Throw in the garlic and tomatoes and sauté another 2 minutes, stirring while it cooks. Add these sautéed ingredients to the onion mixture and stir them in.

11. Add the "pasta" and saved water to the vegetable mix and combine. Add basil and1/2 cup Parmesan and stir. Remove from heat and keep warm.

12. Salt and pepper the chicken on both sides and pour flour in a bowl. Fully coat the chicken with gluten-free flour, and then shake off excess flour in the bowl.

13. Add the lemon juice and broth to the pain and bring to a boil. Cook for 3-5 minutes. Remove from heat, add the butter and the sliced spring onions and stir until the butter melts.

14. Serve the sauced chicken over the pasta. Top with the rest of the cheese.

TOMATO-BACON SQUASH PASTA

GF | P

The smoky taste of bacon is sublime when paired with the earthiness of squash and the sweet tomato ties it all together.

Prep Time: 40 m

Serves: 2–4

Calories: 467, Sodium: 803 mg, Dietary Fiber: 7.8 g, Total Fat: 30.6 g, Total Carbs: 31.8 g, Protein: 11.2 g

INGREDIENTS

....

2 cups yellow squash, spiralized

1 basket cherry tomatoes, halved

4 strips thick-cut bacon, chopped

1 large red onion, chopped

4 garlic cloves, minced

½ cup white wine

1 ½ cup chicken stock

½ cup fresh rocket, chopped

3 Tbsp. olive oil

2 Tbsp. Italian seasoning

....

DIRECTIONS

1. In a large frying pan, fry the bacon. Remove the bacon and drain off all but a few Tbsp. of bacon fat. Add the onion to the pain and cook until it begins to turn golden, then add the garlic and continue to cook.

2. Add the white wine. Deglaze the pan (scraping up the caramelized bits with a wooden spoon and stirring them into the sauce).

3. Add the chicken stock and the tomatoes. Cook for several minutes until the tomatoes are heated through, then add the Italian seasoning.

4. Spiralize the yellow squash into flat rings.

5. Crumble the bacon back into the pan and add the noodles, stirring to combine everything. Add the rocket and cook another few minutes until the greens wilt.

6. Serve immediately.

VEGGERONI & CHEESE

Everybody's favorite comfort food without the gluten or carbs and with an extra boost of green vegetables! Make it quickly on the stovetop or bake it to a crispy goodness.

Prep Time: 15–60 m

Serves: 4–6

Nutritional Info: Calories: 343, Sodium: 360 mg, Dietary Fiber: 2.3 g, Total Fat: 22.5 g, Total Carbs: 19.1 g, Protein: 18.8 g

INGREDIENTS

....

"VEGGERONI"

4-6 courgette or four large broccoli stalks, spiralized

MAIN INGREDIENTS

2 Tbsp. unsalted butter or olive oil

4 Tbsp gluten-free flour

4 cups milk (can use non-fat)

1 9-oz package of Cheddar cheese, grated

....

DIRECTIONS

1. Using spiralizer, create 4 cups of vegetable noodles (flat crescents recommended) and set aside.

2. In a heavy duty saucepan, melt the butter (or heat the olive oil).

3. Add the gluten-free flour and mix to make a "roux."

4. Add the milk and whisk until the milk begins to thicken into a sauce.

5. Add the grated cheese and stir until it melts.

6. Add the veggie noodles and heat through, about five minutes.

7. Serve hot right off the stove, or bake in a greased glass pan at 350 degrees until the cheese gets a little crusty on top (about 45 minutes).

Note: If you've ever used spinach- or tomato-flavored pasta to make Mac n Cheese, you know that kids really like the idea of "green" noodles. Encourage that fascination!

YELLOW SQUASH PASTA WITH SUN-DRIED TOMATOES

This is a beautiful dish with its yellow pasta and deep red sun-dried tomatoes. If you're in a hurry, you can even make it with a bottled salad dressing, just choose one without sugar (harder than it sounds) to keep the calories down.

Prep Time: 15 m

Serves: 2–4

Nutritional Info: Calories: 286, Sodium: 82 mg, Dietary Fiber: 1.8 g, Total Fat: 28.0 g, Total Carbs: 7.0 g, Protein: 4.1 g

INGREDIENTS

....

"PASTA"

4 cups yellow squash (4-6 stalks), spiralized

SAUCE

1 package sun-dried tomatoes, cut into strips

½ cup Parmesan cheese

½ cup olive oil

2/3 cup red wine vinegar

2-3 garlic cloves, minced

1 Tbsp. Italian seasoning

....

DIRECTIONS

1. Spiralize the yellow squash into flat pasta strands.

2. Place the cut-up sun-dried tomato strips in a bowl and cover with boiling water to rehydrate them.

3. Warm the veggie pasta for three minutes in boiling water.

4. Combine the oil, vinegar, garlic, and spices. Pour over the warm pasta.

5. Drain the tomato bits and add to the pasta.

6. Sprinkle with the Parmesan cheese and toss to coat.

7. Serve warm or cold as a pasta salad.

Note: There's no need for added salt with this dish as the Parmesan cheese is quite salty.

COURGETTE PASTA & CHICKEN SAUSAGE

This is a meat sauce that shares top billing with tomatoes and greens. If you're craving the taste of a sausage and peppers sub, substitute 2 diced Bell peppers and a chopped yellow onion for the rocket and enjoy.

Prep Time: 30 m

Serves: 4

Calories: 233, Sodium: 856 mg, Dietary Fiber: 2.6 g, Total Fat: 11.3 g, Total Carbs: 8.2 g, Protein: 27.3 g

INGREDIENTS

....

"PASTA"

2 large courgettes, spiralized

SAUCE

1pound hot Italian chicken sausage

1 Tbsp. olive oil

2 garlic cloves, minced

1 cup cherry tomatoes, halved

3 cups rocket or spinach leaves

¼ cup Pecorino Romano or Parmesan cheese, shredded

1 tsp black pepper

....

DIRECTIONS

1. Spiralize the courgettes into thin strands. Heat or cook to your preferences.

2. Brown sausage in the bottom of a large saucepan over medium heat until it is completely well-done. If bulk Italian sausage is not available in your grocery store, substitute, 4 links of Italian sausage with the casings removed.

3. Stir in the rocket, tomatoes and garlic and cook until the greens are limp and the tomatoes start to break down, about 3-5 minutes. Cover and remove from heat.

4. Mix the cheese with the "pasta" then add the meat sauce.

COURGETTE PASTA WITH AVOCADO SAUCE

The sauce here is so rich, creamy, and nutritious you could almost drink it as a "green smoothie."

Prep Time: 10 m

Serves: 2

Calories: 323, Sodium: 84 mg, Dietary Fiber: 11.9 g, Total Fat: 24.2 g, Total Carbs: 26.5 g, Protein: 7.8 g

INGREDIENTS

....

"PASTA"

4 medium-sized courgette, spiralized

SAUCE

1 ripe avocado

1/2 cucumber, peeled and sliced

¼ cup lemon juice

1 large garlic clove, crushed

2 Tbsp. unsweetened, unflavored coconut or almond milk

Pepper and salt

....

DIRECTIONS

1. Spiralize the courgette into thin strands. Heat or cook as you prefer.

2. Combine the rest of the ingredients in a blender and process until smooth.

3. Mix sauce with the "pasta" and serve immediately.

COURGETTE AND SQUASH NOODLES WITH GOLDEN RAISINS, PISTACHIOS, AND MINT

A light, summery dish, this pairs well with fish or chicken. It can be a good substitute for heavier pasta or grain dishes, in the gluten-free diet. Keep the noodles very lightly cooked for a nice, crunchy texture.

Servings: 4

Prep time: 15 minutes

Cooking time: 20 minutes

Nutritional Info: Calories: 141, Sodium: 42 mg. Dietary fiber: 3.8 g. Total fat: 4.1 g. Total carbs: 25.8 g. Protein: 4.7 g.

INGREDIENTS

....

1 large yellow squash, spiralized

1 large courgette, spiralized

1 Tbsp. lemon zest

Juice of 1 lemon

½ tsp. honey

3 garlic cloves, crushed

1 ¼ cup vegetable stock

1 medium shallot, finely chopped

½ cup golden raisins

¼ cup chopped pistachios

2 Tbsp. chopped fresh mint

Olive oil

Salt and pepper to taste

....

DIRECTIONS

DRESSING

1. Whisk together lemon zest, lemon juice, honey, and ¼ cup olive oil.

2. Add garlic cloves and set aside for at least 30 minutes.

NOODLES

1. Spiralize the yellow squash and courgette into thin strands.

2. Bring the vegetable stock to a boil.

3. Add spiralized vegetables.

4. Boil for 2-3 minutes until just tender.

5. Drain and set aside to cool.

ASSEMBLING THE DISH

1. Heat 2 tablespoons of olive oil in a large frying pan.

2. Add shallots, raisins, pistachios and ½ - 1 teaspoon salt.

3. Toss well and cook 1-2 minutes till lightly toasted.

4. Add cooked noodles, and cook 2-3 more minutes till slightly crispy and golden.

5. Remove the garlic cloves from the dressing.

6. Toss dressing with noodle mixture

7. Sprinkle with chopped mint.

8. Serve at room temperature.

COURGETTE PASTA WITH CHICKEN & CAULIFLOWER

This recipe is surprisingly good, making the extra effort of cooking and blending the cauliflower well worth it. Try this with a garnish of fresh parsley for a classic presentation reminiscent of French country cuisine.

Prep Time: 35–40 m

Serves: 2

Calories: 479, Sodium: 1,318 mg, Dietary Fiber: 15.0 g, Total Fat: 19.1 g, Total Carbs: 37.8 g, Protein: 47.0 g

INGREDIENTS

....

"PASTA"

2 large courgettes, spiralized

CHICKEN & SAUCE

½ lb. cooked chicken, chopped

1 large head (roughly 1.5 pounds) cauliflower, roughly chopped

1½ cups chicken stock

¾ cup mushrooms, sliced

½ small yellow onion, diced

2 garlic cloves, minced

1 Tbsp. Herbes de Provence

2 Tbsp. olive oil

1½ Tbsp. white balsamic vinegar

½ Tbsp. Dijon mustard

½ tsp freshly cracked black pepper

½ tsp sea salt

....

DIRECTIONS

1. Spiralize the courgette into thin strands.

2. Heat 1 tablespoon olive oil in a large saucepan.

3. Sauté the chopped onions and minced garlic until the vegetables are soft and translucent but not brown.

4. Sprinkle with salt and pepper.

5. Add the cauliflower pieces and sauté them for five minutes, stirring to keep them from sticking or burning.

6. Add the chicken stock, stir, and bring to a boil. Cover pan and reduce heat, simmering for 5-10 minutes until the cauliflower is tender.

7. In a medium frying pan, sauté the sliced mushroom in 1 tablespoon olive oil until they're fragrant.

8. Add the cooked chicken pieces and continue to cook until they're warmed through. Set aside.

9. Place the cauliflower/stock mixture into a blender. Add the mustard, vinegar, and Herbes de Provence. Blend until smooth.

10. Add the cauliflower mixture to the chicken.

11. Divide the pasta onto two plates and top with the chicken/cauliflower mixture.

Courgette Pasta with Prosciutto, Snap Peas, Mint and Cream

A new take on a classic dish, the crunchy peas and mint add bright notes. This veggie pasta pairs well with grilled or baked chicken, but is strong enough to stand on its own as a main dish. It can easily be made vegetarian by substituting a bit of butter and a dash of salt for the fattiness of the bacon.

Servings: 4

Prep time: 15 minutes

Cooking time: 20 minutes

Nutritional Info: Calories: 302, Sodium: 546 mg. Dietary fiber: 5.0 g. Total fat: 18.2 g. Total carbs: 23.7 g. Protein: 13.8 g.

INGREDIENTS

....

1lb o r 454 gms courgette, spiralized

4 garlic cloves, minced finely

3 Tbsp. olive oil

¼ pound prosciutto, finely diced

4 shallots, minced finely

1 pint cream

½ cup fresh grated parmesan

½ pound fresh snap peas, whole, coarsely chopped

½ cup fresh mint, chopped

Salt and pepper to taste

....

DIRECTIONS

COURGETTE PASTA

1. Spiralize courgette into thin strands.
2. Bring a large saucepan of lightly salted water to a boil, add courgette noodles and blanche until just tender, 2-3 minutes.
3. Add peas to water, and boil and addition 1-2 minutes till slightly tender but crunchy.
4. Drain well, and set aside.

SAUCE

1. In a heavy sauce pan, heat the olive oil over medium heat.
2. Add the garlic and cook for 2-3 minutes, until just beginning to brown.
3. Add the prosciutto and cook for 3-5 minutes, until beginning to crisp and fat renders out.
4. Add the shallots and cook for 3-4 minutes, until shallots begin to soften and turn translucent.
5. Add several pinches of salt and pepper.

6. Add cream, and bring to a boil, stirring constantly.

7. Add cheese, stir well, and reduce heat to low.

DESSERTS

Sometimes all you need at the end of the meal is a piece of sweet, juicy fruit, or a couple of squares of unsweetened dark chocolate. Sometimes, though, you want something a bit more complex, a bit more nuanced. Or let's be honest, you want something that's just...a bit sweeter.

GF - Gluten-free

P - Paleo

WL - Weight-Loss

V - Vegetarian

Vg – Vegan

APPLE RIBBON PIE WITH NUT CRUST

Gluten-free living means finding alternatives to traditional baked goods. No one will feel deprived by this yummy dessert with its buttery nut crust. Braeburn apples are preferred, as Golden or Red Delicious apples can become mushy. Spiralizing the apples gives them a unique texture.

Prep Time: 60 m

Serves: 1–10

Nutritional Info: Calories: 333, Sodium: 30 mg, Dietary Fiber: 5.5 g, Total Fat: 17.6 g, Total Carbs: 44.2 g, Protein: 5.0 g

INGREDIENTS

....

CRUST

2 cups chopped unsalted nuts (walnuts, peanuts, almonds, pecans)

3 Tbsp. melted unsalted butter (do not use margarine)

1 Tbsp. granulated sugar

FILLING

6 medium Braeburn apples, spiralized

¾ cup granulated sugar

1 tsp. cinnamon

2 Tbsp. cornflour

1 Tbsp. lemon juice

½ cup golden raisins (optional)

....

DIRECTIONS

CRUST

1. Combine ingredients and press into a 9-inch pie pan.

2. Bake at 350 for 10-12 minutes until crunchy but be careful not to burn the nuts.

3. Set crust aside to cool but leave the oven on.

FILLING

1. Preheat oven to 350 degrees.

2. Peel and core the apples and spiralize them into thick strands.

3. Combine the sugar, cornflour, and the cinnamon and mix with the apple ribbons and raisins if desired.

4. Pour into the pie shell.

5. Bake at 400 degrees for 45 minutes to an hour. Filling will be bubbly and a little caramelized.

Note: You can make lovely strands out of any firm fruit, so if you like, substitute firm pears for the apples and add 2 tsp. of ginger to the spice mix.

APPLE & RHUBARB COMPOTE

This recipe comes in both G and R-rated versions. Serve as-is for a homey family dessert, add 1 Tbsp. of Calvados for an adults-only treat.

Prep Time: 40 m

Serves: 6

Calories: 201, Sodium: 30 mg, Dietary Fiber: 5.1 g, Total Fat: 3.9 g, Total Carbs: 43.6 g, Protein: 0.4 g

INGREDIENTS

....

6 Red Delicious Apples, spiralized

4 rhubarb stalks, cut into one-inch pieces

½ cup granulated sugar

1 tsp. vanilla extract

2 Tbsp. butter

¼ tsp. ginger

¼ tsp. cinnamon

....

DIRECTIONS

1. Combine the butter, sugar, vanilla, spices and (if using) the brandy in a large saucepan. Cook over medium heat until the butter is melted.

2. Spiralize the apples into flat rings.

3. Add the apple ribbons and rhubarb pieces to the saucepan mixture. Simmer for another 15-25 minutes until the fruit is soft and the sauce has thickened.

4. May be served hot or cold.

Note: If rhubarb isn't in season, you can substitute 2 Bartlett pears peeled, cored and cut into bite-sized pieces. Increase the ginger to 1 tsp.

GLUTEN-FREE APPLE CRISP

GF | V

This delicious dessert is fast and easy to put together and can be served hot or at room temperature. If you're feeling decadent, top with a little ice cream

Prep Time: 70 m

Serves: 6–8

Calories: 191, Sodium: 45 mg, Dietary Fiber: 5.3 g, Total Fat: 8.1 g, Total Carbs: 32.0 g, Protein: 1.7 g

INGREDIENTS

....

6 large apples, unpeeled, cored & spiralized

1/3 cup almond flour

½ cup pecans, chopped

1/3 cup whole oats (not the instant kind)

3 Tbsp. brown sugar

½ oz butter

1 ½ tsp. cinnamon

½ tsp. ginger

Juice of one lemom

....

DIRECTIONS

1. Preheat oven to 375 degrees and spiralize the apples into flat rings.

2. Combine the apples, 1 teaspoon cinnamon, ginger, brown sugar and lemon juice. Toss until apple ribbons are coated.

3. In a second bowl, combine the almond flour, oats, pecans, brown sugar, and remaining ½ teaspoon cinnamon. Use a fork to cut the ingredients together until the texture is crumbly.

4. Put the apple mixture into a 10-inch pie pan and cover with the "crisp" topping.

5. Bake at 350 for an hour until the filling is piping hot and the topping is crisp and slightly caramelized.

6. Remove from oven and let stand for 5 minutes before serving.

PINEAPPLE PASTA WITH MINTED BERRY SAUCE

This surprisingly sophisticated combination of fruits sparked with fresh mint works as both a refreshing end to a dinner party or as a kid-friendly treat in place of ice cream.

Prep Time: 10 m

Serves: 6–10

Nutritional Info: Calories: 95, Sodium: 2 mg, Dietary Fiber: 3.9 g, Total Fat: 0.2 g, Total Carbs: 24.2 g, Protein: 0.8 g

INGREDIENTS

....

"PASTA"

1 medium, slightly unripe pineapple, spiralized

MAIN INGREDIENTS

1 pkg. frozen raspberries

1 bunch mint, chopped

....

DIRECTIONS

1. Spiralize the pineapple (flat rings recommended). Place in a colander set over a bowl to drain.

276

2. Combine the thawed raspberries and the chopped mint in a blender or food processor until smooth. (If the sauce is meant to be served to adults, you can spike it with a bit of crème de menthe liqueur.)

3. Divide the "pasta" into serving dishes and pour the sauce over the fruit ribbons.

Note: This fruity dessert can be made even simpler by simply pouring fresh blueberries on top of the pineapple.

SWEET POTATO PUDDING

GF

This is a spectacularly satisfying gluten-free dessert for a holiday feast. Substitute coconut oil for the butter and almond milk for the milk and it's suitable for vegans.

Prep Time: 75 m

Serves: 6–8

Calories: 335, Sodium: 204 mg, Dietary Fiber: 3.7 g, Total Fat: 11.3 g, Total Carbs: 53.7 g, Protein: 8.2 g

INGREDIENTS

....

1lb o r 454 gms uncooked sweet potatoes, spiralized

3 eggs, beaten

2 Tbsp. melted butter

2 cups milk (may use low- or non-fat)

½ cup raisins, plumped in ½ hot water and drained

¾ cup pecan halves

1/2 cup dark maple syrup

3 tsp. pumpkin spice mix

1 tsp. cinnamon

....

DIRECTIONS

1. Preheat oven to 325 F.

2. Spiralize the sweet potatoes into flat crescents.

3. Coat an 8 x 8 baking pan with butter or non-stick cooking spray.

4. Combine all ingredients and pour into prepared pan.

5. Bake for an hour.

Note: *This can also be made with squash or pumpkin.*

NEXT STEPS...

DID YOU ENJOY THIS BOOK?

IF SO, THEN LET ME KNOW BY LEAVING A REVIEW ON AMAZON! Reviews are the lifeblood of independent authors. I would appreciate even a few words and rating if that's all you have time for.

IF YOU DID NOT LIKE THIS BOOK, THEN PLEASE TELL ME! Email me at **feedback@HHFpress.com** and let me know what you didn't like! Perhaps I can change it. In today's world a book doesn't have to be stagnant, it can improve with time and feedback from readers like you. You can impact this book, and I welcome your feedback. Help make this book better for everyone!

ABOUT THE AUTHOR

J.S. Amie is "the Healthy Happy Foodie"—a food blogger and Amazon bestselling author who is quickly building a name as a trusted source for delicious recipes which support healthy diets and lifestyles including Gluten-free and Paleo diets. Her books on vegetable spiralizer recipes are gaining popularity with a wide variety of people who all share the same passion for eating well while staying healthy.

She is a mother of two charming daughters, who, like normal children, crave sugar, wheat and more sugar! So what to do? JS decided to learn how to satisfy those urges by substituting good, natural food for unhealthy junk. Her books reflect her personal mission to nourish her family and friends as well as possible. She lives in a small town surrounded by rolling hills, walnut trees and zombies. Just kidding about the zombies.

She can be contacted on her blog at

www.HealthyHappyFoodie.org.

DON'T FORGET TO REGISTER FOR FREE BOOKS...

Every month we release a new book and give it to our readers...absolutely free! This helps us get early feedback before launching a book, and lets you stock your shelf full of interesting and valuable books for free!

Some recent titles include:

- The Complete Vegetable Spiralizer Cookbook

- 101 The New Crepes Cookbook

- The Complete Food Dehydrator Cookbook

To receive this month's free book, just go to

http://www.healthyhappyfoodie.org/a5-freebooks

Printed in Great Britain
by Amazon.co.uk, Ltd.,
Marston Gate.